RAGE AGAINST THE MANUSCRIPT

YOUR GUIDE TO ROCKING SELF-PUBLISHING,
FINDING YOUR READERS, AND BUILDING A
KILLER AUTHOR BRAND

SECOND EDITION

STEFF GREEN

ISBN: 978-1-991349-00-2

❀ Created with Vellum

RAGE AGAINST THE MANUSCRIPT

- Do you have a story you're bursting to tell the world?
- Are you sick of being rejected by the publishing establishment?
- Do you want to inject a little punk rock, DIY ethos into your indie author career?

In *Rage Against the Manuscript*, bestselling indie author and publishing coach Steff Green shows you how to tell your story, find your readers, and build a badass author brand.

As a self-published author you'll learn how to:

- Define your measure of success and set attainable goals.
- Create an exciting author brand you want to write under forever.
- Tame your monkey mind and consolidate your gazillion ideas into a solid plan.
- Choose the best platforms, editors, designers, and tools to create a high-quality book.

- Plan a compelling book series in any genre that will have your readers chomping for more.
- Write faster, release more often, and enjoy what you create.
- Spot trends and gaps in the market where you can add your unique voice.
- Publish your book in print, ebook, and audio with all the nuts and bolts.
- Launch with a BANG! – including handy launch checklists.
- Create an engaging author platform to turn your readers into lifelong fans.
- Find unique and emerging opportunities in self-publishing to build your audience and earn a living.

Steff breaks down the 11-step process that's seen her go from failed archaeologist and obscure music blogger to a *USA Today* bestseller with a six-figure income. With dozens of examples from across the publishing landscape and real-talk from her own career, Steff shows how imagination, creativity, and perseverance can help you achieve your dreams.

Rage Against the Manuscript isn't just a book about writing, it's about grabbing your dreams by the balls, living faster, harder and louder, and cranking your art up to 11.

SO YOU'RE READY TO START SELF- PUBLISHING

You've been working hard to hone your writing chops and create work you're proud of, and now you're ready to share it with the world.

Perhaps you've approached a publisher already and been pushed back, or maybe you have a small audience online and you want to know how to deliver something meatier than a blog post. Maybe you're a storyteller with the dream of seeing your name on the spine of a real book, or perhaps you're excited about the possibilities of making writing your full-time career. Maybe you're all of those things. Or none of them.

Whatever kind of writer you are, allow me to welcome you to the wild, crazy, frustrating, and wonderful world of self-publishing.

Digital reading and self-publishing through platforms like Amazon KDP, Apple Books, and Kobo Writing Life have opened up tremendous opportunities for writers to get their work directly into the hands of their readers. We no longer need a publisher to make a book and get it found. This means we can keep the majority of our royalties instead of sharing them with a big corporation. Because of this, writers all over the world can find their voice and audience, make a profit, and write full-time. It sounds awesome, and it is.

But…

…there's a steep learning curve from being a pen monkey hiding in your cat pile to becoming your own publisher. You're no longer just a writer – you have to be the editor, designer, business manager, marketing department, *and* tea-and-sandwiches person.

What's fantastic about this route is that there are many paths to success – every day I'm amazed by stories of writers making it big and finding their readers in new and unique ways. This book is mainly about my own experience and the things I've learned so far, but I've tried to also include lots of stories about other writers I'm lucky enough to know to show you that you don't have to do things 'my way' to succeed.

I've set out *Rage Against the Manuscript* as a set of eleven… let's call them guidelines. I don't like to call anything a 'rule,' because for every 'rule' I believe exists, I can point to a writer who is killing it breaking that rule. But they are *guidelines* that can help steer you to a path of least resistance and put you in the best possible position to hit your writing and publishing goals. If your ultimate dream is to quit your day job to write full-time, then paying attention to these guidelines can help you get there.

This book is short, but it's packed with information. It's going to feel a little overwhelming – but I hope it will also inspire you to action. What I want to do is show you all the possibilities that are open with self-publishing, and leave it up to you to choose the path that suits you best. Don't feel as though you have to do everything – but you should start with something.

The main thing I want you to take away from this guide is just how possible it is to be a successful self-published author, that there are many different paths to success, and give you some solid next steps for your particular project. Are you ready? Let's get writing!

WHO AM I?

Just so you know that I'm not talking out my arse, I'll tell you a little about my writing career and success with self-publishing.

I'm Steff. I'm a New Zealander. I love to brew my own mead and cuddle my cats, and I'm legally blind. I grew up in a small town with book characters as my only friends. I was a genuinely weird kid who sucked at sports and had an unhealthy obsession with Ancient Egypt... incidentally, I grew up into a weird adult who still sucks at sports and I still have an unhealthy obsession with Ancient Egypt.

Reading was an escape for me, and from a very young age, I wrote stories about worlds I invented and the people who inhabited them.

I wrote all through high school and university, finishing around four full-length novels that were all completely terrible. I sent one off to a publisher's mailing address I got from the back of a Baby-Sitters Club book and received a very encouraging form rejection.

Fast-forward a few years. I went to university to study archaeology. I got a postgraduate degree and volunteered in every museum and for every excavation that came up. When

I finished my studies, I tried to find a job, but after a year of searching, no one would hire me. I was told I was a 'health and safety' risk because of my wonky eyes. After a museum curator said I "couldn't be trusted" around artefacts, I took the bus home in tears.

After about eight months of these kinds of rejections, my husband couldn't bear to see me continue to put myself through this farce of trying to prove I *could* work. He suggested I consider a different career path. "If you look at it this way, you've done archaeology. You've been on all these digs and achieved all these cool things other people don't normally get to do. Maybe you could think about what you'd like to do after that – and it should be something where no one can say, 'You can't do this.'"

As soon as he said that, my mind went to those half-finished novels saved on my hard drive. I always wanted to be a writer. It was something I could do by myself, without someone hovering over me waiting for me to fail.

But I didn't know how to become a writer. I had no idea how writers earned money or what I should do next. Did I have to go back to university? Who hired writers? Did I possess the requisite number of cats?

I did what any self-respecting Millennial would do. I Googled 'how to make a living from your writing' and proceeded to try everything on the list.

I pitched articles to magazines. I started a blog. I wrote product descriptions for gothic corsets and glittery wall paint. I got my first cheque for $10.50 for an article I wrote. Then another for $25, for $55, for $180. I kept pitching magazines, offering my services to businesses, and selling myself. I learned that I couldn't take rejection personally because then I could never move forward.

I never gave up.

Most importantly, I pulled out an old novel and finished it. I pitched it to an editor at a writer's conference, and she asked to read it. I felt as though I could taste my dream. Just one final hurdle, one more gatekeeper, and I'd be there!

But the publishing world moves slowly, and interest is not the same as a book deal. After working with that editor on three different manuscripts over five or so years, I was finally close when the editor retired, taking my hopes of a publishing deal along with her. I was devastated. So many years of work and I'd have to start all over again.

Yet again, someone had told me, 'You can't do this.'

Around that time, writers like Hugh Howey and Amanda Hocking were talking about how well they were doing self-publishing ebooks on Amazon. I decided to take one of my trunked novels and self-publish that to see if I liked the experience. It was a terrible book that sold exactly 122 copies, but I loved editing it, designing a cover and promoting it. I loved that no one told me I couldn't do it.

I was hooked.

Next, I started to self-publish the Engine Ward series of weird science fiction books, in both paperback and Kindle editions, under my name S C Green. They sold okay – 5-10 copies a month or so, but I didn't feel like I was any closer to my dream of being a full-time writer.

One day, I attended a party where a friend and I were discussing *50 Shades of Grey*. This friend loved the books, and I'd read the first chapter and couldn't continue because of the writing style.

I was being a typical 23-year-old and bitching about this book's success when my friend cut in to say, "It's not as if you could write a sexy book like that, Steff."

I nodded in agreement and changed the subject because she was right. I wasn't being supportive of another woman's success or about my friend's tastes. Also, in my group of sexually adventurous friends, I'm known for being the one who can't say the word 'penis' without blushing. Of *course*, I couldn't write a book like that.

Of course not.

I mean, c'mon.

But in my head, the cogs were turning.

Challenge accepted.

In secret, without telling anyone, I wrote a 30,000-word story about a fox shapeshifter named Ryan who lived as a reclusive artist, and Alex the gallery curator who brought him out of his shell. There's a shifter war and an unhinged brother and a crumbling medieval manor and all sorts of murder and chaos and intrigue. I'd never had so much fun or found the words came so easily.

I paid $50 for a cover from someone I found on the internet and published *Art of Cunning* in April 2015 under a secret pen name – Steffanie Holmes. I expected nothing to happen except that one day when I wasn't so mortified about the sex in it I could show it to my friend and we'd both have a laugh.

I sold 1,000 copies in the first week.

I couldn't believe it. I kept expecting Amazon to call me up and say they'd given me someone else's royalties by mistake. But they never called, and the sales kept coming. I had to sheepishly tell my husband that I'd made all this money from my books, but it wasn't from my super-serious science fiction I'd been writing for a decade, but a smutty fox shifter romance story I wrote in less than three weeks.

After he was done laughing, he said, "Are you going to write more?"

(Spoiler alert: I wrote more).

Fast-forward to now. I've published over 50 books, most of them kooky, spooky romance novels as Steffanie Holmes. I quit my day job in Feb 2018 to live the dream life of a full-time writer. I earn seven figures a year from my writing and have the most incredible fun doing it.

I am so insanely lucky and grateful, and that's why I've written this guide – because I want you to be able to share in the joy of telling stories of the heart and seeing your writing find an audience.

MY SELF-PUBLISHED BOOKS

The same week I left my day job, I released my first whychoose novel, *The Castle of Earth and Embers*, book 1 of the Briarwood Witches series. Whychoose, in case you don't know, is a romance trope where the heroine falls in love with not one but three or more heroes who all love her back. In the end, instead of choosing one of them, she has a happily-ever-after with all of them. Whychoose became a trend in 2017, with many books hitting the Amazon bestseller lists around the time I wrote this book.

Up until this point, I'd been doing well off the back of my previous paranormal romance novels, but it's thanks to the Briarwood Witches series that my career started to take off. It felt like a sign from the universe that I'd made the right decision.

Before the release of *The Castle of Earth and Embers*, I was earning between $2,000-4,000 per month on Amazon, and about $500-1,000 on the other stores. Since I started releasing the Briarwood Witches books, my income climbed to $4k, $6k, $10k, and up.

I released 5 books in that series throughout 2018, approximately 1 book every 2 months. Each novel was around 80-100k in length. In December 2018, I released the box set of the complete series.

In January 2019, I released *A Dead and Stormy Night*, book one in another whychoose series – the Nevermore Bookshop Mysteries. What's been interesting about this series is that it doesn't follow the typical conventions of a romance book. I planned it based on a cosy mystery plot but with reverse harem elements. It was a gamble, but that gamble paid off – the Nevermore Bookshop series has been even more successful so far than the Briarwood Witches, and it's so much fun to write.

In May 2019, I noticed a lot of readers on Facebook groups asking for 'bully romance' books. I'd never heard the term before, so I read a couple and got completely hooked. I never planned to write one, but one day the idea for *Shunned* came to me in a dream. I dropped everything, wrote a blurb and made a placeholder cover, put a pre-order up on Amazon, and then wrote the book in 3 weeks. This book just poured out of me – it reminded me of the time I first tried writing romance. I felt like I was on to something magical.

I was right.

When *Shunned* released, it hit 45 in **the entire Amazon store**. It stayed in the top 100 for five days. In 30+ books, it's the first time I've ever had a real hit, and this series changed my life. It's introduced my writing to tens of thousands of new readers and has enabled me to step up my career in a big way.

And I followed it with the biggest flop of my career.

After I finished writing the four-book Kings of Miskatonic Prep series, I thought I'd keep going with bully romance, and write something dark and gothic and twisted. What came out of my spooky brain was the Manderley Academy series – a love letter to my favourite gothic writers - and too much of a genre mishmash to appeal to readers.

With Manderley book 1 tanking, I decided to pivot again. Most bully romances were contemporary, so I'd write contemporary…that has to work, right?

So I went contemporary.

For the next two years, I wrote 16 dark bully romance novels, trying to replicate the success of Kings of Miskatonic Prep. It mostly didn't work, but then Tiktok came along. I started making little videos about my books and also testing scenes and ideas for my upcoming series…and this worked. My new series, *Poison Ivy*, launched in the top 300 and shot me straight back up to Kings of Misktaonic Prep levels. I started work on book 2 and figured out how I could spin off more characters to keep the readers engaged.

…and I was unhappy.

The truth was, the success of Poison Ivy made me realise I didn't want to write dark romance. I'd said all I wanted to say about those kinds of characters, and the settings and stories didn't interest me any more. I wanted to go back to the lighter, quirky style of the Nevermore Bookshop series, which has always been the series closest to my heart and the one I wished had done better than it did.

In a magical twist, the *week* I made the decision that this series would be my last dark romance, and I'd be writing more books in the Nevermore Bookshop world, I had my first ever viral Tiktok, shooting Nevermore Bookshop book 1 back into the top 500 for two months.

It felt like a sign from the universe.

In 2023, I slowed down my release schedule and put out the whychhose Grimdale Graveyard series, set in a town next to the village in the Nevermore Bookshop series. Truthfully, this new series has never done amazing, but it's a solid earner that leads people into the Nevermore Bookshop world.

In 2024, I had another moment where it felt like the universe was speaking to me. I decided to write a new series – the Nevermore Murder Club and Snutty Book Coven. I deliberately made strategic choices to make this series as appealing to a 'mainstream' readership as possible. I used popular, clear tropes, and I made it MF instead of whychoose. My decisions paid off, because book 1, Fangs for Nothing, has become one of my bestselling book 1s and resulted in interest and an exciting book deal from a traditional publisher. (But that's a wild story for another book NOT about self-publishing).

I'm telling you this history because, throughout this book, I'll be referring to my own books. They are my most readily available sources for examples and learning. You might like to read them to see how I put the lessons in this book into practice to create a seven-figure income self-publishing. I'll also refer to other books and authors, and to resources to help you along the way.

Getting to the point where I wrote my resignation letter took 3 years of serious work, 25 self-published books, and a stubborn refusal to be disheartened by my approximately 7 million mistakes. Now my audience is bigger than ever, and I'm doing amazing projects like launching $200k Kickstarter campaigns, having a series published traditionally, and speaking at and attending reader and author events around the world. I'm working every day from my home library buried under a mountain of cats. I'm not going to lie – it's a very nice life.

I want you to have the success you dream of. I want you to be able to tell your stories and find the readers who need them. I want you to build a sustainable long-term writing career (if that's your dream) and give back my knowledge and enthusiasm to a community that has given me so so so much. That's why I wrote this book. I hope you get something out of it, and out of the self-publishing experience. It's been one of the most rewarding things I've done in my life – may it be so for you.

Steff

WHAT EVEN IS SELF-PUBLISHING?

BEFORE WE DIVE into the nitty-gritty details of how to do the thing, let's talk about what self-publishing is and what it isn't, as well as the history of self-pub. I promise the good stuff is coming, but I think it's worthwhile looking at the context of self-publishing before you dive in.

Otherwise, it would be like reviewing a new Iron Maiden album without ever listening to *The Number of the Beast*.

When an author self-publishes, they're bringing their book to market themselves, instead of going through a publishing house. The author is responsible not just for writing the book, but for making the cover, finding editors, formatting a manuscript, and finding a way to get it into the hands of readers. The author might do these things themselves or outsource them, but the key to self-publishing is that the author **retains control** over the process.

Self-publishing has been around for a long time. British satirist Laurence Sterne self-published the first two volumes of *Tristram Shandy*. Nathaniel Hawthorne, Emily Dickinson, Walt Whitman, and Jane Austen all experimented with self-publishing their work. Self-publishing of pamphlets and zines has been key to most underground movements throughout history, from occultists in the 17th and 18th centuries to political movements, activism, and the punk and heavy metal music scenes.

In the 20th century, self-publishing was mainly referred to by a derisive term – 'vanity press.' It used to be that if you were an author who'd exhausted the options for having your book traditionally published, you only really had a few options left. You could toss your manuscript under the bed and write something else, you could look for a small press, or you could pay a vanity press a large sum of money to print thousands of copies of your book, which you'd then have to hand-sell to readers.

Many of these self-publishing companies are little more than scam artists preying on the desires of authors to see their work in print. They often send 'acceptance' letters to potential authors, explaining their work has been 'selected' for publication and will be printed as soon as the invoice is paid. These authors had no understanding of how the publishing industry worked and assumed this was how all publishers operated. They'd happily fork over their $10,000 to have a box of books printed which they would then foist upon sympathetic friends and family.

Because of this, if you said 'self-publishing' to an industry professional, it would conjure up images of a well-meaning writer selling boxes of poorly edited memoirs, poetry books, or religious treatises from the trunk of their car. Self-publishing was a dirty word, not discussed in polite company, and certainly not a threat to the status quo.

Very few of these vanity press books made it big on the mainstream. Those that did were usually non-fiction books from authors on the speaker circuit. They'd print a book to sell at the back of the room after their talks, and as their audience got bigger and their ideas spread, traditional publishers saw the potential for their work to reach a wider audience and picked up those books.

Two pieces of technology have transformed self-publishing in the last twenty years. The first is print-on-demand technology. This is where books are printed one at a time as they're ordered. As a reader, I place an order on Amazon for a book. Amazon then prints one copy of that book and sends it out to me. The author doesn't have to set up a website or fulfilment system – they just collect a royalty.

POD books have enabled authors to sell print books with little to no overhead while removing the tricky fulfilment process. The downside is that POD lacks economy of scale, which means the books tend to be priced higher than traditionally published books that can be printed in bulk and are often of lower quality. This matters less than you might assume for reasons I'll get into next.

The second thing that changed self-publishing was the Kindle. Ebooks existed before the Kindle (which also wasn't the first e-reader on the market), but they were usually sold as PDF documents to be read on a computer screen. This worked for some non-fiction publishers, but it was hard to convince readers to enjoy fiction on a screen. You couldn't curl up in front of the fire with a cup of tea and a computer monitor, and since most websites were free, people didn't see why they should pay for digital content.

Some specialist publishers like Ellora's Cave (which sold erotic ebooks for women as downloadable files and thrived in the 90s and early 2000s) found success in the digital market. Ellora's Cave understood that women didn't want to read books with racy covers and titles in public, but they would do it on their lunch break or when their families were in bed. Most free erotic content on the internet was written by men for men and didn't give women what they were looking for. Ellora's Cave served a niche, and they made it their business to understand what their audience craved. We're going to be talking about niches throughout this book.

Despite Ellora's Cave leading by example, most publishers

couldn't capture online readers with PDFs and expensive ebooks.

What the Kindle did when it launched in 2007 was give readers the ability to enjoy digital books in the same way they currently enjoyed their print books. It appealed to ageing and print-disabled readers who liked the ability to enlarge print, and to travellers and commuters who wanted a portable library. It offered an e-ink screen that recreated the experience of print, without the eye strain of a screen's glare.

Originally, only a few books were available to readers in the Kindle store. Many publishers thought it was a fad and didn't bother adding their books to the Kindle library. Amazon wanted to offer readers more options. They realized they'd never be able to sell Kindles if they couldn't offer anything for readers to actually *read*. They needed to fill their library with more content, and when they couldn't get that content from traditional publishers, they launched KDP Publishing to allow any writer, anywhere in the world, the ability to create and publish an ebook with no upfront costs. They decided to sweeten the deal by offering something no publisher would ever be able to do – authors publishing through KDP could keep 70% of the list price as royalty if they priced their book between $2.99-$9.99.

Early on, some enterprising authors realized their work could fill gaps in the ebook market for hungry readers. In 2010, Amanda Hocking decided to put her rejected paranormal YA books up for sale for $0.99 each, and 18 months later she'd sold 1.5 million copies. Midlist thriller author Joe Konrath started self-publishing his out-of-print titles and found himself moving 1,000 units a day. These authors wrote about their experiences online, and more and more authors joined KDP.

By 2011, ebooks were firmly established as part of the reading landscape. The New York Times added an ebook bestseller list in both fiction and non-fiction (which is now gone, but that's a story for another day!) Self-publishing success stories started to spread, and more authors jumped on board.

Amazon changed the market again in July 2014 by launching Kindle Unlimited, a subscription program where voracious readers can borrow an unlimited number of books each month for a flat fee – KU is Spotify for books. Instead of being paid a per-book royalty, authors with their books enrolled in KU are paid for every ebook page read.

All was great in the digital world… or was it? Readers rebelled against digital books and started buying expensive print books in droves. Or did they?

You might have seen articles like this one from *The Guardian*, or this one from *Forbes*, or this one from *Mental Floss*, explaining how digital books have fallen in popularity as readers lust after the bygone days of print. These articles make trad publishers feel good. They are… sort of true. But also not true at all.

The writers of their pieces rely on data taken from Nielsen, who record book sales for each ISBN. That data shows that fewer people are reading digital books, as the sales of ISBNs on digital books have decreased. There's no denying that.

However, you don't need an ISBN to self-publish your books on Amazon. Many self-published authors don't use ISBNs because they can cost money and be a hassle to procure. Here in New Zealand, we get ours for free. In other countries, you pay as much as $100 per ISBN, and you need a new ISBN for each format. Many authors don't bother with ISBNs. Self-publishing success is going unnoticed and uncounted by the wider industry, which means they struggle to react.

The data also doesn't cover a vast quantity of self-published books. The most comprehensive studies have been compiled by a site called Author Earnings, associated with the author Hugh Howey (another early self-publishing success story) and his data-loving friend known only as 'Data Guy.' Author Earnings has unfortunately disappeared from the internet, but many of the results are still available from secondary sources.

Author Earnings analyzed data about online book sales, including self-publishing stats as far as they can be extrapolated from publicly available Amazon data. Their work showed that 65% of fiction readers prefer reading digitally, that Big 5 publishers account for only 18% of digital sales, and that self-publishers own 40% of the total ebook market. That's 40% of the market that isn't counted in Nielsen stats. Far from declining in popularity, this section of the digital market – the self-published books – **is growing and taking market share every year**.

Certain genres will always have a huge print market – coffee table books, children's picture books, literary fiction, etc – and it's important as an author and publisher to understand how people in your genre are reading your books. You may be surprised to learn that it's digitally.

Who is reading all these ebooks? Most self-publishing success stories are from genre fiction – crime, thrillers, romance, mysteries, horror, science fiction, and fantasy. If you're writing in one of these genres, you are already on the way to success. If not, don't fear – it may take a little bit more imagination and ingenuity, but there will be a way to find your readers.

SELF-PUBLISHING AND PRINT

While most successful self-published authors focus on genre fiction in ebooks, some have found success with print, especially since the rise of Booktok in 2020.

Print success for indies (independent authors – another name for self-published authors) doesn't usually mean following the traditional model of finding a distributor and getting books into bookshops. Some do this, but it can be difficult to find a distributor who deals with indies, and if you do, they may require a large volume. Their discount plus the bookstore discount when combined with the higher per-unit price of POD books often means this is barely profitable for the author.

However, bookstores aren't the only place where readers buy print. Many of the most successful print-focused authors I know are public speakers or other figures who have established an audience.

Gala Darling is a blogger I've followed for years. Gala built a platform on her blog with her fun posts about fashion and creating outfits that made her smile. Over the years she pivoted from being a fashion blogger to talking about self-esteem and a concept she created called 'radical self-love.' She amassed a following of thousands of rabid readers. Before self-publishing through KDP was even a thing, Gala started writing a book about radical self-love and releasing a chapter every month. Her readers could grab each chapter for $10 and get a PDF and an audio track of Gala reading the chapter aloud.

According to Gala, she made $100k selling her book in this way. She decided to edit the chapters together into a proper book and pitch it to publishers. She couldn't get anyone to offer her a deal, so she self-published *Radical Self Love* through KDP – she only had a paperback version available, but her fans snapped it up and sent her soaring to the top of the self-help and metaphysical categories. Her success caught the attention of Hay House, who offered her a publishing deal.

What's unusual about Gala's story is that she didn't even self-publish an ebook version of *Radical Self Love*. She knew most of her loyal readers had those early chapters stashed on their hard drive, and wanted to push them to a physical product. Gala's self-publishing experiment worked because she spent years building her audience online. Gala has since self-published more books and recently launched a YouTube show and app. Gala's story shows how powerful an engaged audience can be, and the power of constantly creating new and useful things for that audience.

I know a great number of authors who've had success launching books via crowdfunding on Kickstarter. These are often books that can be given as gifts – children's books, art/photography books, or journals. Often they have a geeky theme or focus on some niche area in the book industry where traditional publishers won't touch.

Have you ever heard of Littlest Lovecraft? They're two artists who created children's picture books based on H. P. Lovecraft's cosmic horror stories. They are freaking adorable, but this is something a publisher never would have picked up. But by taking their books straight to Kickstarter, they were able to find an audience. Each of their five Kickstarter campaigns has raised between $25-45,000.

Also on the Lovecraft theme, I picked up a cookbook called the Necronomnomnom from Kickstarter. This was a cookbook designed to look like an ancient magical tome, complete with calligraphy and esoteric doodles on every page. It's as much a piece of art as it is a cookbook, and it appealed to the geeky audience of Kickstarter, who backed it to $80,000. For a project like this, readers want to own the print version (and sometimes even the deluxe limited edition version) and will pay a premium for the privilege.

And let us not overlook one of the most popular Kickstarters of all time – *Goodnight Stories for Rebel Girls*. The authors started off creating apps and app magazines for kids, but after the market slowed, they worked with a traditional publisher on a series of six picture books. This series didn't go as well as the authors anticipated, but they loved creating books, so they decided to focus on publishing themselves through their own company, Timbuktu Labs, and to focus on building their audience online. They brought a lot of knowledge from the start-up world to build their community and market their books.

Their books telling inspiring stories of real women in a fairy-tale format have sold more than 3 million copies. Read more about the authors and their thought processes around the books here.

BOOKTOK, DIRECT SALES, AND SPECIAL EDITIONS

When I started writing a 2024 update for this book, I knew I'd need to talk about Booktok. In certain genres (including mine) Booktok has completely changed the way we market our books to readers.

During the pandemic, people were bored and stuck at home, so they signed up for the Tiktok app and the algorithm served them fun little videos about stuff they like. And lots of people like reading, so they watched and made videos about the books they liked (and books they hated). And Booktok was born.

Booktok serves a new generation of readers. These readers are hungry for books in their favourite genres, and unlike those of us who embraced the ebook revolution, they love physical books – especially pretty books they can display on their shelves like serial killer trophies.

Indie authors – especially romance authors – are always the first to engage with new ways of reaching readers. So authors started to create their own booktok videos about their own books and saw those videos go viral. Caroline Peckham and Susanne Valenti (aka, The Twisted Sisters) were two early adopters of TikTok who went viral with a "You loved Harry Potter but wished it was spicy…" video that catapulted them to the top of the Amazon charts. You can see a video where Caroline talks about their TikTok strategy here.

As word spread and readers and authors flocked to the platform, Titktok became an amazing way for authors to get their books in front of an audience of voracious readers. And authors started to realise that they didn't need bookstores to sell print – readers would buy from them directly, especially if they could purchase limited edition, fancypants books signed by the author.

These books also do well at live events, like signings and conventions.

Now, many genre fiction authors (especially in romance and fantasy) have a hugely profitable business built from direct sales, special edition books, and short-form video content. I'm one of them. It used to be that 99% of my earnings came from ebook royalties from Amazon, but now around 40% of revenue is from direct sales (Kickstarter campaigns and my website) of special edition hardcover books.

I'm going to talk more about how to create special edition books in a later chapter.

Other areas where print can do well:

- Any book you can sell at events you're already involved in, such as art books for gallery shows, comic books and graphic novels for cons, and professional speakers selling books at the back of the room.
- Adult colouring books. Collect 20 related original line images together and publish on thick paper.
- Poetry books that reach a specific audience. Many poets sell print copies and chapbooks at events and build a community on social media to push their books.
- Creating your own magazine/workbook. Kat Williams of Rock N Roll Bride self-published a glossy bridal magazine based on her blog content. Check out an interview in *Cosmopolitan* magazine for her tips.

- Limited edition hardback versions of your books for collectors, perhaps including special paper types, embossed covers, or illustrations.

AI AND SELF-PUBLISHING

Yes, we have to talk about AI.

AI has burst onto the publishing scene in a big way in 2024. Whether you're excited by the possibilities, staunchly anti-AI because of the way it steals from artists and the environmental impact, have no idea what's going on, or are somewhere in the middle, we must talk about things that impact our industry so you understand your options.

At the time of writing, AI is not yet able to produce a full-length fiction book that a human will enjoy reading. That hasn't stopped unscrupulous people flooding Amazon with AI-written books in an attempt to get rich quickly. No one is buying these books in the same way that no one was buying all the other get-rich-quick attempts on Kindle over the years, so I don't personally worry too much about this.

I do worry about other things, though. Likely, AI will eventually be able to write a serviceable – although formulaic – novel. AI can currently create pretty decent cover art, marketing copy, and TikTok videos (although it does depend on what you're asking it to do) and the current AI we're seeing is the worst it's ever going to be. AI will only improve and as authors, we need to figure out how to navigate it.

AI is already being used in the industry in several ways, some of which you may be interested in or brush up against:

- Most translators will use AI to do a first pass on a manuscript, converting it from one language to another, before going over it again to make it sparkle and correct all the AI errors. The conversion process is the most time-consuming aspect of translation, so using AI to assist them with this means translation costs for authors can come down.

- AI can create images and videos that might more exactly match your book's story without being expensive (for example, creating a video of a dragon in flight for a fantasy series).
- AI can act as a springboard for ideas. You can type in "Give me twenty ways to solve a locked room murder mystery" and maybe something on the list will solve your plot problem.
- AI can help you generate marketing copy for Facebook ads and TikTok videos.
- AI can create an audiobook using a synthetic voice for a fraction of the cost of hiring a voice actor and producer.
- New AI startups targeting authors are offering a range of tools, including market research, book discovery, manuscript wrangling, and marketing services.

Sounds great, right? Not so fast. There are many issues with the use of AI:

- **Currently, anything created with AI is not copyrightable.** There is a lot of ambiguity here (what about a book where a single scene is written with the help of AI, or a translation where AI has assisted, etc), but until we have more case law this is a legal grey area that's going to cause a lot of issues for authors.
- **AI is trained on stolen work.** The AL algorithms don't come up with content to train their engines on their own – Books3 is a dataset of nearly 200,000 pirated books that have been used to train AI, most of which have been published in the last 20 years

and are not out of copyright. AI companies like OpenAI (creators of ChatGPT) have argued that it would be impossible for AI to exist without using copyrighted works. They care about the technology more than they care about the creators they're ripping off, which makes AI morally wobbly for creatives to use.

- **Some readers are anti-AI.** While I believe most readers don't care, those who *do* care are loud and will rake you over the coals publicly for the use of or non-disclosure of AI. This may not harm your bottom line but it can impact your reputation.
- **You risk alienating other creatives.** The artists, narrators, illustrators, and designers I work with have been particularly hard hit by AI use. I think they're amazing and I want to keep paying amazing creative people to make cool shit for me, so I will continue to be a company that works with humans. Excessive use of AI, especially from creators who can afford to do otherwise, can lead to being ostracised by your peers.
- **AI has a high environmental toll.** Powering AI engines requires a huge amount of energy. The data centres that house AI deployments require massive amounts of raw material and rare-earth elements to produce, produce electronic waste (including lead and mercury), require staggering amounts of energy to run, and may soon consume more than 6 times more water than the entire country of Denmark.

How you choose to use AI – or not – is completely up to you. No judgment here. I'm not a big AI user. I don't like to draw a line in the sand and declare "I'll never use this thing," because the technology is new and the copyright law is still mostly untested, but at the moment I haven't seen much use for AI in my business, and I love my human creator friends too much.

As for worrying about your books not selling because AI-generated content flooding the market, my view is that building a fandom is the one protection authors and other creatives have against AI taking our jobs. What we deliver to the marketplace is a unique voice and human connection that AI can't replicate. Lean into this and carefully and strategically build your fandom.

This is easier said than done, but I'm going to try and show you how to get started throughout this book.

THE FUTURE OF SELF-PUBLISHING IS WIDE OPEN

Every day I read or listen to stories of self-published authors finding their readers and seeing success. This industry hasn't even scratched the surface of what technology and innovation will make possible in years to come.

The only question you have to ask yourself is whether you want to join us in the trenches. Are you ready for the wild ride of publishing your work and taking your stories to the world?

Enough of my rambling – let's get into it!

CHAPTER 1

FIGURE OUT WHAT SELF-PUBLISHING SUCCESS MEANS TO YOU

WHAT ARE you trying to achieve with self-publishing?

Answering this question impacts every subsequent decision you make about your writing, from what book to write and which distributors to choose, to how and where to market. Are you:

- Wanting to disseminate information and ideas, or raise your profile within your industry? (By writing a non-fiction book on your topic of expertise).
- Producing a family history book? (To chronicle the lives of your ancestors for posterity).
- Using a book as an additional tool to showcase your other creative work? (For example, a photographer compiling their work into a tabletop art book. A chef creating a cookbook to sell at their cafe).
- Breaking into a new market? (A commercial illustrator producing their first children's book).
- Wanting a physical product to sell at events? (If you're a motivational speaker or poet).
- Fulfilling a lifelong dream to tell wonderful stories?

- Using publishing as a motivational tool to force yourself to finish your writing projects?
- Writing for creative pleasure and to see a copy of your book on the shelf?
- Wanting to write books and make a little extra money on the side of your day job?
- Trying to make a full-time living as an author?

Every one of these reasons is totally valid and completely achievable. There's no value judgment on who you are or what you want out of your writing. We're talking about this now because you gotta know your **metric for success** before you dive in.

Why? Because this book is all about rocking self-publishing – i.e. being successful. But 'success' is a nebulous term that means completely new things to each writer. Every section of this book is designed to give you ideas to build your rocking plan, and you can't build a plan if you don't know what that plan is pointing towards.

An author who wants to publish their family history will have a completely different idea of success than a writer who wants to quit their day job. The artist who wants to create a quality book for their collectors will have a different approach from the fantasy author who wants to pitch their series to Netflix.

My approach for this book deals particularly with getting your writing to as many people as possible and making a living as a self-published author. This was my primary goal when I started pursuing publishing ten years ago, and that's the goal of most of the peeps I interact with.

In saying that, many of the techniques and ideas will work just as well no matter your endgame.

I want you to be aware if you're feeling overwhelmed that my success metric is different from yours, and that's okay.

Only you can decide your measure of success. It's most

likely obvious to you, as it's the driving force behind your innate *need* to write. No one is forcing you to work on this writing project instead of watching TV, so why are you doing it? Because you have a story inside you burning to get out? Because you think other people would find your information useful? Because your fans/followers/customers have been asking for it? Because you believe your writing will create a better life for your family? Because you want to change the world? A combination of all of these?

Answer the why and you'll arrive at the heart of your measure of success.

A lot of people burn out from their creative pursuits because they don't ask themselves what brings them joy. I know this from personal experience.

I enjoy drawing and painting, and although I've never been professionally trained, I do have some skills. In my 20s, I tried to set myself up as an illustrator. I thought it would be a great sideline to writing and help me to land more work. So I spent my evenings creating pieces for an illustration portfolio, working on a children's book, and reading articles about being a professional illustrator. I even started pitching myself to some publishers and had a bit of interest.

It was fun, for a while. That it was too hard. One day I found I couldn't bear to sit in front of the easel any longer. The idea of painting *repulsed* me. I resented the fledgling sideline I'd built for myself. I thought all my work sucked. I wanted to tear my drawings up and never show them to anyone ever again.

I'd taken the joy out of drawing because I never sat down to ask myself *why* I liked to draw. And when I did that reflecting, I discovered that I had no desire to draw commercially for clients based on *their* briefs. I liked doodling things that made me smile. I found satisfaction in completing a drawing, mastering new skills, and hanging a painting on the wall in our home or giving it away as a gift. But I didn't want to run an online store and deal with bad reviews and a social media presence and limited print runs and pitching for publishers. That wasn't fun to me because I'd let my real passion – writing – dry up amongst all that other stuff.

Don't let this happen with your writing.

I'm a big believer that your creative pursuits should be insanely, joyously *fun*. They should make you excited to get home in the evening, they should occupy your thoughts in the shower, they should be a celebration of who you are and what you stand for. There are literally a million easier ways of making a living than following a creative career. That's a fact – a million easier ways to make them sweet dolla bills. I'll count them if you want to wait.

No? You sure?

Let's say I'm right. There are lots of easier ways to make a living. Not all of them will be enjoyable, but if the end goal is riches, who cares?

You care – because you want to write. Because writing and telling stories is fun.

Why pursue a writing career with no guarantees of fame and fortune if it's not fun?

Some of us enjoy the creative challenge of simply finishing a project. Others are lit up by creating something for their existing fans or presenting their current creative passions in a new way. You might be drawn to the rush and validation of winning contests and prizes, or you have ideas and stories you want as many people to enjoy as possible. You might be like me and you want to create a body of work that makes you proud and offers something good to the world. Also, like me, writing might be the only thing you want to do all day and you enjoy the challenge of building your income to a point where you can quit your job.

Look at the writing and other activities you already do in your spare time. What occupies your thoughts? What excites you and fires up your imagination? What do you work on when no one is forcing you to work? This is where you'll find what you're truly passionate about.

Think of what you're trying to achieve with your project. What lights you up?

- I want to see my book in print.
- I want to create something I'm proud of.
- I want to create a fun product that my followers/fans/customers will love.
- I want to win literary prizes and awards.
- I want 20,000 people to read my book.
- I want to see my book on the shelves in bookstores and libraries.
- I want to spread ideas/stories that will change the world.
- I want to help pay the bills with my writing.
- I want to make a full-time living from my writing.

Now that you know your success metrics, if possible, put some solid numbers on it. What's your timeline? What numbers are meaningful to you? If you want to finish your family history, then your goal could be to complete research by the end of the year and have a first draft completed by next July.

If your dream is to make a living as a writer, what does that mean? What monthly income do you have to hit? When do you want to hit it? Figure that out and start building a plan to work toward it.

For me, when I set this goal, I wanted to earn 75% of my current salary, and I had a year to do it. I'll tell that story a little later in the book.

I'm not going to do a whole chapter on SMART goals, because we've all heard the lecture a thousand times and we know the acronym – but you should be making your writing success goals as SMART as possible. If you want a refresher, there's a great article about SMART goals for writers on the *Happy Self-Publisher*.

LITERARY ACCLAIM OR A MILLION DOLLARS?

The fiction book world is firmly divided down the middle into two separate teams. A select few books occupy a nebulous space somewhere in the middle, but they're the exception. Most of us sit firmly on one side or another.

Literary: According to *The Guardian*, "Literary writers are the luxury brands of the writing world...these people are smarter than you, so you should buy their book." Literary fiction is often introspective and focuses on wider issues important to humanity. Its purpose is to make you think. Literary fiction is what ends up on award lists and taught on a university syllabus. (I include most poetry in the literary category).

Commercial/Genre: This is what the majority of people read. These are books to scratch an itch – familiar stories and characters that make you happy. Although genre fiction can and does tackle the world and the human condition, its primary purpose is to entertain. Genre fiction includes crime and thrillers, science fiction and fantasy, historical, and romance.

Generally speaking, if you seek acclaim, then you go in the literary direction. If you want money, you want to think about genre. You can think about non-fiction writing similarly. There's non-fiction written for acclaim, and non-fiction written to entertain and inform. There's no value judgment here – you have to decide for yourself where your talent and passion lie.

Generally speaking, genre fiction will do better self-published. This is because genre readers don't make as many value judgments about *the publisher of a book* as literary readers. Genre readers choose books that look entertaining from their preferred category, whereas literary readers rely more heavily on reviews from certain publications and award lists (that won't accept self-published work), and the quality standard of their favourite publishers to make their buying decisions.

If you're a genre writer, self-publishing has great potential to help you reach your dreams. If you're writing non-fiction that entertains and informs, you're also in a great position as people looking for information don't tend to care where it comes from and how it's delivered as long as it's engaging and answers their questions.

If you believe you're a literary writer, then think carefully about your goals and success metrics and whether self-publishing is the right way to reach your readers. It's possible, but it's going to be hard work, and you've got to laser-focus on your readers' habits and preferences and be more creative in how you reach them.

HOW TO ROCK YOUR SUCCESS METRICS:

- What does success as a writer mean for you?
- Imagine yourself five years from now. (If this feels too difficult, narrow it down to one year from now). Picture yourself as a writer. What does that look like? How many books have you published? What genre? Do you write full-time? Are you selling poetry books at an event? Who are your readers? What does your writing contribute to the world? What have you created? How do you feel about your career? Describe your dreams and visions in the past tense, as if it's already happened. Knowing where you want to be will help you see where you should focus.
- What have you already done to move toward that dream? Make a list of all the projects you've

completed or are half-finished on your hard drive. What about writing groups or social networks you participate in? Awards you've won? Craft books you've read? Look at this list for patterns and proclivities.

- What's an immediate goal that will get you closer to your ideal future? Is it finishing a book, publishing a project, launching a new pen name, or creating an author brand?
- Are you a literary writer or a genre writer?

CHAPTER 2
YOU NEED MORE THAN ONE BOOK

HERE'S THE THING – books hit the market with gusto. They get lots of attention during their first few months of publication, and then reader interest wanes as soon as more shiny new books hit the shelves.

If you want a sustainable long-term career as an author, you need more than one book. The more new releases you have, the more you'll get to hit that 'new release spike' and capture more fans who'll go back to buy all your previous books.

There are exceptions, of course. Harper Lee made her career off a single book. But I always choose not to believe I'll be the exception.

(As I said previously, I wrote this book based on my experiences and my personal success metric – which was to become a full-time author and make enough to pay the mortgage and keep my cats in the manner to which they've become accustomed. If that's not your goal then some of these tips may not apply to you, especially this one).

In indie publishing, you only have to sell 1,000 books a month with a $4.99 price tag to make an average wage (average here in New Zealand, anyway). You'll earn a 70%

royalty for each book sold at that price point, so you can do the math to see how many books you'd need to sell each month to pay your bills. Don't forget to also factor in taxes, health insurance, and a savings cushion!

For an average person, I estimate the magic number for a sustainable career is around 1,000 books per month. That may seem like a huge number to hit if you only have one book (especially as that book will fall in popularity over time), but when you have 5 or 10 or 20 books in your backlist, your 1,000-book target becomes achievable. Add audiobooks, paperbacks and other income streams, and you'll be rocking your way to the bank.

Instead of imagining your one book hitting bestseller lists and paying for a fancy mansion (or even just a studio apartment these days), think about what you want your career as an author to look like. What kind of books do you want to be known for? How will they all fit together? Will you write for kids or adults? Are you a commercial or literary writer? Do you write series or standalones? If a reader was talking about you to someone, how would they describe you?

This is what people talk about when they talk about your 'author brand.' It can help to break your brand down into a simple sentence that describes what you do. For example, my brand for Steffanie Holmes is 'kooky, spooky romance.' Every book I write under that pen name fits in some way into that brand, as does any promotion I run or social media post I make. I always want readers to be able to pick up one of my books and visit one of my homes on the internet and know what to expect.

The 1,000 books a month system is only going to work if each book you write builds on the success of the others. Each book helps you grow your audience and then offers them *more of the things they like*.

(More on this in a sec).

You don't have to do this 'branding' exercise if that kind

of thing gives you hives. It's just useful to have a sense of where you're going so you can get excited about your future projects and direction. Also, being consistent with what you give your audience will help you build a sustainable career and reach your success metrics sooner.

AUTHOR BRANDING

This is overly simplistic maths, but say you have ten books out and they're all psychological thrillers, if you can get 100 readers interested in just one book, then those 100 readers will potentially buy all 10 books because they love psychological thrillers. You only need to find 100 readers to hit your 1,000-reader goal.

If, however, you publish one psychological thriller, one closed-door small-town romance, one epic fantasy, one western, two YA fantasies, and then a spicy rom-com…then for each book you need to attract a new audience.

This is because of the way readers choose books. Here are some things you might not know about readers:

- Generally, readers stick to one genre (or even one subgenre). As authors, we usually read widely across a range of genres, but readers tend to stick to one small section of the bookstore. Even my readers will say, "I read widely. I like contemporary romance and paranormal romance and sometimes even a little bit of dark romance."
- Readers are series-loyal first, genre-loyal second, and author-loyal a DISTANT third. The more voracious readers are within a genre, the less likely they are to be loyal to an author because they want more of the same experience over and over.
- Genre fiction readers are often voracious readers. They might read and purchase books in multiple

formats – ebooks for daily reading, audiobooks while they're at work or in the car, and paperbacks or hardcovers to collect. They are the perfect audience for self-publishing authors.

- Readers generally prefer books with a protagonist who matches their gender and basic demographics, although there's lots of variation here. This is because of a common reader habit of imprinting themselves onto the main character. It's easier for a reader to imagine themselves as a main character if they have similar life experiences.

- For this same reason, readers are often harsh on the "likeability" of their main characters in their reviews, especially in women-led genres like romance (because of patriarchy). The reader doesn't like to read about a character who is "bitchy" or "antisocial" because they don't like to imagine themselves with undesirable traits.

- Readers are looking for safety in their books – an experience they can predict and have control over. Readers pick up a romance because they want to experience falling in love, and a mystery because they want to feel their heart race and solve a complex puzzle. Giving your readers a safe, reliable experience is how you build a brand and a career.

- Readers often say things that aren't true, especially in reviews and surveys. Readers will yell at you about how much they hate cliffhangers at the end of a book, but if you end book 1 on a cliffhanger, they are more likely to buy book 2.

- **Readers tell us what they want through their buying habits.** Trust the data over what readers say.

An example of this last one might be this: you're a

romance writer and you have a reader group. You ask your readers what they want to read from you next, an epilogue book following your most popular couple after their happily-ever-after or a brand new story in a popular trope. Your readers overwhelmingly want the couple's story because they loooooove this couple, so you do it…and it doesn't sell.

I've been resident in Romancelandia long enough to know it's not going to do well because readers SAY they want to see more of a couple, but a book about a couple who's already had their happily-ever-after isn't going to be a romance unless you break them up first and no one wants that. Any author who has done this has data to show it doesn't work. Listen to the data.

So, now that you know more about readers, you can start to figure out what you want your author brand to be. Talking about 'branding' can feel corporate and boring. And after I did that big spiel about how I believe your writing career should always be fun!

I know, I know, but branding is an important thing to get a grip on if you want to make a career of this or if you're writing books as part of a wider strategy. Besides, it is kind of fun. It's a thought exercise on how to distil the essence of YOU into a fun little package.

Branding isn't a logo. It isn't a website or a style guide. Branding is **making and keeping a promise to your readers**. Good branding says, "You can trust me. I promise I'm going to give you exactly what you want every single time."

A solid brand is why people return to fast food restaurants like McDonald's again and again. You know that no matter what city you're in anywhere in the world, you can walk into a McDonald's and purchase the same thing and it will taste identical. It's trustworthy in a world where very few things feel dependable.

You already have an author brand. You don't even have to do anything! Because a brand isn't something that you *do* –

it's the way people see you and how you make them feel. Readers already make judgments about you and your work based on what you put out in the world. Now that you know this, you can take control. Your brand may be reader-defined, but it is author-influenced. The way you package your books, your words, and yourself will enable you to influence the brand you want.

Your brand is a billboard telling the world who you are and what you stand for. It allows other people who enjoy the same things and agree with what you stand for to easily identify you. Actively tweaking and controlling your brand gives you the power to find and attract these readers.

You may think it's too early to be thinking about this stuff. You might be right. It depends. On what? **On your success metrics.**

If you're trying to publish a memoir so you have something to give your grandma for Christmas, your brand doesn't matter so much. If you want to be a full-time successful self-published author, then your brand matters a hell of a lot. The sooner you nail a consistent brand, the sooner you can put the other tips in this book into action.

HOW DO YOU CREATE YOUR AUTHOR BRAND?

The first step is to understand who you're writing for. Who are your readers? What are their likes and dislikes? How old are they, where do they live, and what gender do they identify as? How many books do they read in a month, and how do they like to read them? The more you know about your readers, the better you can craft your brand and your books to fit their desires.

Knowing this stuff doesn't mean you have to hire a market research firm or tarot card reader. For some genres, there's already reader demographic information available. Just search online and you'll find lots of great info about reading habits. If you can't find anything, you'll need to dig around to uncover what you need.

One of the best places for researching readers in your genre is TikTok and Instagram. Follow book influencers in your favourite genres and pay attention to how they talk about books, what they like, their favourite tropes, and their demographics.

You can also look at blogs, discussion boards, and reader groups for books in your genre. Check out the reviews on a popular book – how much demographic information can you glean from those? Talk to readers of your genre and pay attention to how. Look at authors you love and study how they use their brands to appeal to certain types of readers.

Once you know who you're talking to, you need to figure out what you want your brand to say to them. How do they like to be spoken to? What words and imagery appeal and what is a huge turn-off? Look at how other authors speak to their readers and take lessons to apply to your brand. We call this 'brand voice.'

Penny Reid is a great example of an author brand. Her books are romantic comedies for women. Everything about her public persona speaks to this brand. Her book covers convey the genre and tone. Although she has lots of different books, they're all designed to appeal to the same reader. Even if you took her name away, they're instantly recognizable as Penny Reid covers. Her tone on her website and social media is bright, breezy and funny. You won't see her going off on a political rant. She doesn't suddenly surprise readers with a dark noir suspense book or a romantic hero who dies at the end – readers know what to expect when they pick up her work. That's why they love her.

Think about what you want readers to expect from your brand. Going back to the earlier example, when we go to McDonald's, we know exactly what to expect. It's not gourmet fare, but it has a taste all of its own, and that familiarity is comforting.

What can readers expect from you? How long will your books be? Will they be a series or standalone? How often will they come out? Will you work on multiple series at once or finish them one at a time? How much access will they have to you via social media? How will they be notified when you put out a new book? Will your brand encompass projects that aren't writing?

No matter how you decide to brand yourself, part of your brand should always be to put out books of high quality, with excellent editing, that are joyful to read. We'll talk a bit more about this later.

WRITERS AND PEN NAMES

Your pen name – whether it's your real name or something invented – is the keystone of your brand. It's how readers recognize you. The tighter the brand of your pen name and the books you publish under it, the more sell-through you'll get from one book to the next, and the faster you'll get to that magic 1,000 books a month. We're going to talk more about sell-through later. For now, think about how you will tie your books together under a pen name.

We've talked about how a consistent brand is important, and how readers like to rely on you giving them the same kind of story. What if you want to write lots of different things? You want to write historical romance! And cookbooks! And dog-walking manuals! And YA fantasy! You have three options:

1. You can throw everything you do up **under one pen name** and hope that some readers will like everything and the rest won't get annoyed at the lack of consistency. The advantage of this is that

you only have one pen name to deal with, and you can use covers and titles to indicate genre. The main problem with it is that when a reader looks at your backlist, they'll feel confused by all the different options. They don't know what they're getting. They will be less likely to read through other books you've written than if you stuck tight with one genre. Also, you'll probably struggle to gain traction in Amazon's algorithms because it will be difficult for the bots to understand what you write and who will want to read it.

2. You can separate each different genre into a **new pen name or identity.** You might put your cookbooks under one pen name, your romance under another and your YA fiction under a third name. The advantage here is you'll have tighter branding and higher sell-through on each pen name. The disadvantage is that you'll have to manage multiple pen names, publishing schedules, marketing, and social media profiles. It will be tough to keep up, and inevitably, you'll end up favouring some names over others. You'll probably see slower progress than if you focused on one single name and genre. If you do choose this option, I recommend focusing on one pen name for several releases to build momentum and backlist before switching between them.

3. You can find ways to tweak your concepts and interests to **incorporate passion projects under one main pen name.** For example, if you have a historical romance series where the heroine is a cook for a fancy estate, perhaps you could create a cookbook based on the series to sell to fans. The advantage is that you can have fun doing all the creative things you enjoy while building a strong,

dedicated fanbase that knows what to expect. The disadvantage is that you might not be doing exactly what you want in the way you want it.

3 is the option I strive for because I want to avoid spreading myself thin across multiple pen names if at all possible. I've followed this in my career. For years I've wanted to write a mystery series – specifically, a cosy or traditional mystery set in small-town England. Doing so would mean starting an entirely new pen name, and I didn't want to do that. Instead, I wrote the Nevermore Bookshop Mysteries series – mashing up the mystery format with a steamy reverse harem romance plot. I got to write my mystery series without having to start a new pen name. And thanks to the popularity of this series, I now get to write fun spooky cosy spicy mysteries all the time.

Another author who does this well is historical author Libbie Hawker. Historical authors are usually branded according to the era they write in, but Libbie has been able to indulge her passion for multiple historical periods through her brand – often by focusing on periods and historical personalities that aren't well-covered by other historical writers. Libbie's work might appeal to a smaller audience, but she's able to dominate underserved niches and respond to trending reader interests.

HOW TO ROCK YOUR AUTHOR BRAND:

- Your brand isn't about a single book. It's the promise you make to your readers. Branding is attached to your author name and encompasses not just the books you publish under that name, but your entire author presence both off- and online.
- You already have an author brand. Branding is the images and associations created in a reader's mind

when they hear your name. With a little work and strategic thinking, you can control that brand to be in line with your **success metrics**.

- Can you sum up your brand in a single sentence? You don't have to tell anyone the sentence, but thinking about your brand as a simple catch-phrase can help you to quickly assess if a decision is on-brand for you or not.
- Who are your readers? Know them and design your brand to appeal to them.
- How will your brand help you to get to your ideal author career? Look at how other authors in your genre manage their brands. Don't stop at visual cues like logos and cover fonts – look at how they speak to readers, how they set a publishing schedule, what they talk about on social media, and most importantly – how their brand makes readers *feel*.
- Pen names – will you have one? How many will you use? How will you manage each name and what will each brand contribute to your success?

CHAPTER 3

CONSIDER A SERIES

AS A SELF-PUBLISHED AUTHOR, you wear three hats. I reckon they're quite trendy hats, but then, I do like hats.

You wear your **writer hat** to get the words on paper. This is a super-creative hat that may not be very good at keeping the rain off, but it will turn heads if you wear it around town.

Once the book is finished you have to take that hat off and put on your **publisher hat** and your **marketing hat**. Your publisher hat is safe and boring, but it keeps your head warm and it's super comfy. Your marketing hat is trendy and sophisticated and perfectly compliments your outfit. However, you bought it on a whim and it probably cost a bit more than you're used to. You don't trust your marketing hat. It seems too ostentatious, too *out there*. Donning it makes you a bit nervous because it's not something you'd normally wear, but as soon as you step out, people exclaim over how awesome it looks.

(The more you wear your marketing hat, the more comfortable it gets. One day you won't even remember feeling nervous about it at all).

All this talk of hats is just my roundabout way of

explaining if you're going to self-publish, as well as being an awesome writer you are now also your own publishing house *and* the marketing department of that publishing house. Most of us don't know how to do either of those things.

Becoming a publisher is the easier bit. You get a free account on Amazon KDP or Kobo Writing Life or whichever platforms you like, follow the steps, and at the end, you have a book!

But when it comes to marketing, you probably feel a little overwhelmed. Most of us haven't marketed a product in our lives, much less a book containing our heart and soul and at least three of our organs. Later in this guide, we'll talk about how to market your published book.

Right now, I'm sharing a little tip about how to plan for success with your self-publishing marketing before you write a single word.

Truth time – a series of connected books in the same world is easier to market than standalone stories.

Why? Sell-through. Readers become invested in the characters and stakes in book one. A certain percentage of those readers go on to buy book two, and a certain percentage of *those* readers will buy books three and four and so on. Remember what we learned about readers earlier – readers are series loyal FIRST.

Using this model, if you get enough people to read book one – even if you **lose money marketing that book** – you can make a profit on the people who progress through the series.

Indie authors like me can calculate our sell-through on a series and see which books perform better than others, or if there's something making readers put down a series before the end.

When I release a series, I expect to see around 50% sell-through to book 2 (half the readers who finish book 1 will pick up book 2), 50-65% sell-through to book 3, and then **90-95% sell-through** from book 3 onward. This means if you're making enough money from each launch in a series, you can keep adding as many new books as you like and you'll know roughly how many sales to expect.

Bestselling romance author Bella Andre uses this logic. She's been writing her Sullivans series since the start of her career. She's now sold over 8 million books with over 20 titles in the series. She knows that if she keeps putting out Sullivans she'll have a guaranteed number of readers for each new release.

Sell-through is much harder on standalone books. Readers have to become invested in a brand new set of characters every time. Readers are series loyal first and foremost, which is why many readers will only read the most popular series by an author and not their other works. Not everyone who reads the Harry Potter books also read JK Rowling's 2012 tragicomedy *The Casual Vacancy* (even if they consider Rowling one of their favourite authors).

There are other advantages to writing in series. Sales platforms like Amazon and Apple Books help to promote your series by making sure readers are alerted to the next book. You can bundle series books together into a box set, which is a great way to draw in new readers. Box sets are an effective marketing tool because they command a higher price point (for example, you might combine 3 books that retail for $3.99 into a $9.99 box set) and only require one sale instead of three.

Having a series also makes it easy to establish your author brand, as the series title and cohesive covers quickly establish you as a particular type of author.

However series don't work in every genre, and because of everything we've already talked about, you should write the kind of book that readers expect to read. Some readers (and especially certain genre readers) are not series readers. Also, you might not be a series writer. We're all different and some of us like writing a story that wraps up in one book.

If you want to write standalones, that's awesome. They can be a good option (and a competitive advantage):

- **Standalones are one and done.** The story is complete in a single volume. This means that you can move on to a new story – can work well if you struggle to follow through with a longer series or you like to jump around different ideas and worlds.
- If the book is a flop, you're not locked into writing more in that world. You can quickly move on to something else, whereas a series author can be locked into finishing a poorly-performing series so they keep their reputation as a writer who finishes what they start (ask me how I know).
- **A massive tome = a massive payout in Kindle Unlimited page reads.** Standalones in some genres (such as fantasy or whychoose romance) can end up longer than individual books in a series, giving you a massive KU payout (if you're in KU – more on this later).
- **The shorter format may inspire you to try something a little riskier that you might not want to do for a full series.** As indie authors, we're free to experiment and take fun risks!
- **Standalones are expected in certain genres:** For example, horror, psychological thriller, and women's fiction are most often standalone books. It can be difficult to create a series in these genres while also meeting the expectations of your readers.
- **Standalones can be profitable. They just take more experimentation.** I know lots of amazing authors who do very well with standalones. It's going to be harder for you to make your ads

profitable, but ads aren't the only way to sell books. With strong hooks you may do well with social media, or by setting standalone books in the same world you may inspire stronger read-through, or you may do well with subscriptions or Kickstarter or…

No matter what you write, there is a strategy out there that will enable you to get your book into the hands of readers. Whether you write series or standalones, it will take time and experimentation (and probably a few books) to find the strategy that works for you.

TYPES OF SERIES

Series work well for fiction, non-fiction, and even poetry. There are many different types of series you could try. I've invented some fun titles so you can remember the different types.

EPIC SERIES (WITH CLIFFHANGERS)

An epic series is where you split one giant-ass story into several books. Each book follows the same cast of characters through their trials and perils. The tension and stakes will usually increase in each book so that by the end of the series you've got some kind of epic showdown.

Each book in your epic series should have a satisfying arc that answers some of the questions raised during the book, even if the story itself continues. If you're clever, you'll end each book in your epic on a cliffhanger to entice readers to continue. Readers will often say "I hate cliffhangers," but their behavior says otherwise. If you use cliffhangers in your series you will usually have better sell-through (and more moolah!), but poorer reviews. Up to you which one you prefer.

Some examples of epic books are *The Hunger Games* by Suzanne Collins, *The Lord of the Rings* by J. R. R. Tolkien, and my own Briarwood Witches series.

THE BAND OF BROTHERS SERIES

This is the series format most commonly employed by romance writers, but I've seen it in other genres, too. I've named it a Band of Brothers because although each book would include a new romantic pairing, one member of that pairing (usually the guy in MF romance – but they don't have to be men!) is part of a close group of other characters – this might be a family group (actual brothers), or it might be a wolf pack, a law firm, a football team, a motorcycle club… the possibilities are endless.

This series format enables you to introduce the other 'brothers' (connected characters – not necessarily men) in the first book so the readers get hooked on them and *need* to know how their stories turn out. Often, but not always, a Band of Brothers series will have an overarching storyline or mystery that will stretch across multiple books, but the responsibility for finding the next clue in the mystery will be passed to the new POV characters.

Bella Andre uses the Band of Brothers format for her popular Sullivans series, as does pretty much every other romance author. JA Huss creates an interesting Band of Brothers dynamic in her Turning dark romance series, where three rich friends keep a string of women locked in a dark room. I use this series type in my Nevermore Murder Club and Smutty Book Coven series, but when I write whychoose books I prefer an Epic Series format.

THE ADVENTURES OF... SERIES

In this series format, you meet the main character in book one, where they will have an adventure that will be neatly wrapped up by the end of book one. In book two, they'll begin another adventure.

Readers continue to devour The Adventures Of… books not because they need to know what happens, but because they're obsessed with the main character and the world you've created.

This is the most popular series format for mystery and thriller books. Think about Kathy Reichs – her books are standalone stories, but they're connected by the main character or set in the same location. There may also be an overarching series arc, but it will usually move much slower than other series types.

Another of my favourite authors who rocks this format is cosy mystery writer H. Y. Hanna. I've not only fallen in love with her main (female) protagonists but also the delightful settings and cast of quirky characters she uses to populate her worlds.

I also use this format in my Nevermore Bookshop Mysteries series, although I also employ mild cliffhangers to keep the ongoing mystery alive.

TUNE IN NEXT WEEK SERIALS

Serials are a very specific type of fiction – usually written like the book form of a TV show. They're released in short instalments on a regular schedule – usually a few days or a week apart. Readers know exactly when they can expect a new episode, and they enjoy reading a short part of a story in one go.

During the Victorian Penny Dreadful era where many

people got their fiction fix from short fiction, serials were a popular format. Charles Dickens made his name writing serials. They fell out of favour as reading habits changed and readers could purchase more lengthy works cheaply.

Thanks to digital reading, serials are seeing a resurgence. Readers are now less tied to considering the length of a book when they choose what to read, and the low price points of digital books make purchasing individual episodes of a serial (or reading them in Kindle Unlimited) affordable.

Popular self-published series have included H. M. Ward's Arrangement series, Luke Jennings' *Codename Villanelle*, and Sean Platt's work. Serials usually won't do as well as full-length novels (there are fewer readers interested in the format) but many serial writers find they do quite well if they release regularly, particularly when they bundle episodes into boxsets readers can binge at once.

TRUST ME - I KNOW WHAT I'M TALKING ABOUT SERIES (NON-FICTION)

You may be thinking, "These series ideas are all well and good, Steff, but what about if I write non-fiction?"

As a non-fiction writer, you can still take advantage of the power of the series.

If you write narrative non-fiction or memoir, then understand that in terms of plot and marketing (if not content), these act in the same way as a fiction series. It's common for narrative non-fiction to be presented as a series and the use of cliffhangers and other tools to encourage readers to pick up future books. Jean Sasson's *Princess* books are a classic example.

If your books don't fit this model, you can still use series branding. Think about overarching ideas or themes that will spread across all of your books. Can you group your books together into topics that would appeal to the same type of person?

A great example of non-fiction series branding is Tim Ferriss, author of bestselling book, *The 4-Hour Workweek*. Tim developed a unique way of running a business and managing his time so that he only had to work four hours a week. When he released his next book, *The 4-Hour Body*, he took a subject matter that was completely different and framed it within his same formula to create a natural progression between the two books. He used the same branding to promote *The 4-Hour Body* and a subsequent book *The 4-Hour Chef* to his existing audience.

THE PRETTY BOOKSHELF...SERIES

"Okay, sure, but riddle me this!" I hear you cry. "I'm a *poet*. How do I create a series for poetry? Do I even need a series?"

To which I reply, you don't need a series. Because these aren't rules – they are guidelines to help you rock self-publishing. But as you've learned, a series is a great way to make your life easier in terms of marketing your work, building lifelong fans, and selling more books.

A poetry series works differently from other books. If you create epic poems in a saga format you could create an ongoing series narrative (The *Odyssey* was the sequel to the *Iliad*, after all). But probably most poets aren't doing that and most poetry readers aren't looking for that experience. (I don't know – maybe they are! You gotta find out).

The key comes in thinking about who your readers are and why they like to buy poetry. Poetry lovers enjoy beautiful language that evokes a place, time or feeling. They also adore the aesthetic joy of words and books as objects. Poetry is among the few self-published genres where the majority of your readers will want a print copy. They want to put it on their shelf and admire it as an *objet d'art*.

More than any other genre, a poetry book should be a pleasure to hold. Look at self-publishing options that allow for different paper and binding types. You could perhaps consider hardback or linen. You may like to do a cheaper version and a deluxe edition with a higher price point for collectors.

Can you find ways to thematically join your collections? Use series branding to create a cohesive look. Your readers will feel as though they need to collect all the books. Also, group poems into collections by type and link the titles together in a similar way. Look at how publishers sell poetry collections as a series and borrow inspiration.

As you'll probably sell a lot of print books at poetry slams and readings, consider doing a small print run locally as well as a POD version for online sales. You can do both versions with the same ISBN.

The Pretty Bookshelf series could also work for authors of standalone books in the same genre. Collect four of your domestic thrillers together into a box set with a slipcase and call it the After Dark Collection or something. Standalone books do great in special edition Kickstarter campaigns and through a direct sales store.

HOW TO ROCK WRITING IN A SERIES:

- Can you find a way to pivot your current project to be a series?
- What series types are most popular in your genre?
- Look at how other authors use branding to link books into a series. Cover, blurbs, themes, tropes, subtitles, characters, settings… how you can learn from their success? What branding elements can you incorporate into your series?
- To cliffhanger or not to cliffhanger, that is the question.

- If you write standalones and you want to keep writing standalones, be strategic about the techniques you choose to focus on. Paid advertising might be more difficult for you but something like social media or Kickstarter may give you a competitive advantage.

CHAPTER 4
RELEASE AS OFTEN AS POSSIBLE

IF YOU ARE TRYING to make a living as an author or get the most eyes on your work, then the more often you release something new, the more opportunity you give yourself to earn a livable income.

This is not a hard-and-fast rule. Of all the guidelines I talk about in this book, releasing often is the wobbliest. I release less and make more money now than I did when I published 8 books a year, but when you're trying to establish yourself and scale up quickly, there are some benefits to being able to write and publish faster and build a backlist.

If you pursue traditional publishing, your publisher will probably only want to release one book by you per year. Research into reader habits has led publishers to adopt this strategy – believing that more than this means your books are competing against themselves for readers' money. Also, publishers only have a limited amount of resources to dedicate to each author. Books are expensive and readers only have so much fun money, and your publisher doesn't want them to have to choose between two of your titles.

Publishers also have a longer lead time to get a book to

market, and they simply don't have the resources to dedicate to an author publishing more frequently.

You might be able to get two publishing deals from different publishers and release two books in a year, but those books will be in different series and you may run into problems with non-compete clauses in your contracts.

Now, this is changing, especially as more publishers are picking up indie authors. When I got my publishing contract, it was for three books that would be released 6 months apart. But that is picking up an existing series from an established author. It is the exception. I never like to assume I'm going to be the exception. If you go trad, expect one book a year.

If you're indie, you can publish as many books as you like.

The rise of digital reading and cheap ebook prices means that voracious readers can devour many more books per month than they could afford to when print was their only option. This explains the success of Amazon's Kindle Unlimited – the 'Spotify for books' where readers pay $10 per month to read as many books enrolled in the program as they like. (You'll be learning about Kindle Unlimited in excruciating detail later).

This lower average list price has brought out what the industry likes to call 'whale' readers. These are voracious bibliophiles who read 1-2 books a *day*. Because of the high price of print books, they're used to relying on libraries to fuel their desire for more books, all the time. Now, they're able to purchase more titles outright.

Most whale readers quickly made the switch to digital reading as soon as Amazon improved the selection available. They tend to obsessively stick to a single genre, and they love Kindle Unlimited. They don't care whether a book is self-published or traditionally published as long as it's entertaining and hits the tropes.

In genres where these 'whale' readers hang out – which are commercial genres such as thrillers, mysteries, romance, science fiction, fantasy, and women's fiction – self-published writers are making a killing by publishing often with low prices.

We also make higher sell-through because if a reader is devouring two books per day, in a year they will have forgotten your first book. But if I can give them the next installment in a couple of months they'll be so happy and excited.

Because self-published authors keep a high percentage of our royalties (70% on books priced between $2.99-9.99 on Amazon, as opposed to 10-25% off the net in a traditional contract) we can afford to price low. Because we're only paying ourselves and we have low overheads (no office space to rent or staff salaries to manage), we can bank most of that as profit. A self-publishing success often looks the same as a traditionally published failure (most big publishing houses need to sell 50,000 copies of a book to make a decent profit. If I sell 3,000 copies of a book, I make over $10k. To a traditional publisher, 3,000 books sold wouldn't even earn out an advance. If I write 8 books a year and make $10k from each book release…)

As I've said before, you only have to sell 1,000 books a month with a $4.99 price tag to make an average wage. That may seem like a huge number of sales to achieve if you only have one book, but when you have 5 or 10 or 20 books (your backlist) the target becomes reachable. The quicker you create a backlist, the quicker you can learn how to write books readers love and earn big.

Also, if you release more often, you don't have to sell as many books with each release to create a viable career. If each book you release sells around 3,000-5,000 copies, one book per year won't be enough to live on, but what about 2-10 books per year? You can see how many self-publishers have thriving careers by rapid releasing.

This is why many self-published authors have made

successful careers in sub-genres and niche audiences traditional publishers won't touch. A higher profit per book means we can create a viable career from smaller numbers. Authors who write successfully in a niche can also build a dedicated following of fans who are desperate for stories traditional publishers can't give them. We're going to be talking about niches all through this book.

(An aside: How do you pronounce niche? I've always said 'neesh' but I've heard so many writers say 'nitch.' That makes my teeth grate, but I'm curious about your thoughts.)

One great example of self-published authors rocking a niche is the fiction genre of LitRPG (Literary Role-Playing Games). Portal fiction into a game world has been big for decades, and the modern genre of LitRPG came out of Russia and went mainstream with a successful traditionally-published book – *Ready Player One* by Ernest Cline. However, self-published authors have made the genre their own. The books read like the experience of levelling up in a video game – you beat up monsters and baddies, grow your experience, and acquire better gear (and usually, a harem of lusty wenches). LitRPG has a growing fanbase of gamers who enjoy these books, but it's generally not something a traditional publisher looking for the next bestseller will publish as the audience is small.

Rapid releasing is a strategy, and like all strategies, it's going to work for some writers and not others. It has served me well during the early years of my career, where I put out 6-8 books a year and was able to teach myself to write faster. This skill enables me to quickly jump on a trend or idea, to test tropes and niches and "fail fast" if something isn't working, and to keep my income relatively steady with constant new releases.

But rapid releasing isn't all sunshine and roses. I started to find that I was so focused on getting the next book written that I barely put any effort into marketing a new release. That worked for a long time, but I realised that I was stifling my growth by not allowing my books time to find new readers in the market before I moved on to the next thing. Publishing another book is one way to grow, but it's not the only way. I got to a point where writing fast was costing me money because of the opportunity cost of not having time to do other things.

Rapid releasing can also be hard on the part of your brain that does all the creative work. You're constantly pushing to get words out with no breaks. This is why a lot of authors will burn out on this method. The trick is to go at a speed that works for you while honing the skills you need to produce a book quickly, and not to compare yourself to others. I'll never be able to write 12 books in a year, and I'm okay with that.

In 2022 and 2023, I moved down to four books a year. In 2024, I did three books. It's 2025 now, and my publishing schedule is wobbly because of my trad pub deal, but I'll likely write 3-to 4 books in 2025, but not all of them will be published.

As a self-published author, you're the CEO, and you get to decide the strategies you adopt. But it's important to talk about speed in self-publishing because it's one of the success factors that enable us to compete with traditional publishing.

HOW TO RELEASE FAST

The release schedules of some authors can seem insane. Cosy mystery writer Amanda M. Lee has for years released a full-length novel every week. I've had years where I've written and published a book every 6-8 weeks.

Don't let those numbers scare you. No one is saying you have to do that to succeed. Plenty of authors make a decent living and grow their audience publishing 3-4 books a year. That's only writing around 750 words per day. For most authors in most commercial fiction genres, 3-4 books a year is doable (of course this depends on lots of factors).

Maybe even hearing '3-4 books per year' sounds terrifying. Maybe you've been fiddling with your novel for five years already. Maybe you think it's impossible you could ever find more time to write and increase your speed. I'm here to tell you that it's 100% possible, and something you should consider doing if you want to succeed as a self-publisher.

Writing is like a muscle – the more you exercise it, the stronger it becomes. It took me five years to write my first novel. And that was dedicating a ton of time each week to butt-in-chair writing. The next I wrote in two years. The next, six months. Now I can write and publish a novel in 6 weeks (although I prefer a more leisurely pace now). The more you write, the more you learn about your writing and publishing process. After a few books, you have it down to a finely tuned machine.

If you want to learn to write faster, there are a few things you can do:

CARVE OUT MORE WRITING TIME

You have a job, a family, kids, hobbies, charity work, and other commitments. We all do. Finding time to write amongst all that can be tough.

If you want it bad enough, you will do it. Why? Cuz if you're a writer, then writing is the most fun you could imagine. If you're not feeling energized and excited about writing at least some of the time, then I'm not sure I can help you (a bit more on that later).

All things being equal, basic math suggests that if you have more time to write, you'll get more written. That's not strictly true because of reasons we'll get into, but it can be true. It's definitely worth giving it a go.

Think about where in your day you might be able to fit in

some time. Can you go somewhere quiet for 20 minutes on your lunch break? Do you have an hour at the end of the day before the kids get home from school? Can you get up earlier and write before the rest of the house wakes up?

Over the years, I became somewhat of an expert at fitting in writing around my day job and other commitments. I don't have kids and I'm not looking after elderly relatives, so keep that in mind. I'd write on my lunch break. I'd write in the evenings. I'd get up early on weekends and write before my husband arose and started cooking bacon. In my final year of working a day job, I would write hunched over my laptop on the bus to/from my tech startup job. I'm not going to lie – it kind of sucked, but it enabled me to work that super-intense job with the horrendous commute while also publishing six books in a year.

If your family is supportive of your writing, ask them to help you find the time you need. This might mean getting your partner to watch the kids for an hour on a certain day, setting aside funds to allow you to go out to a coffee shop to write once a week, or renting a hotel room for a weekend to escape into your book.

WRITE IN SPRINTS

Now that you've found a few pockets of time to write, you should maximize what you're able to achieve in that time. Maybe you're thinking, "What's the point of having 20 minutes to write if all I do is stare at a blank screen?" The answer is – fill the screen with words.

Many writers find sprints effective for focusing their writing time and filling the screen. To 'sprint' you set a timer for a short period. I find 30 minutes perfect for me, but you can experiment with anything from 10-45 minutes. As soon as you press GO, start writing. Don't stop. Don't think. Don't look at Facebook. Just write until the timer goes off. When it does, you're allowed a break for a couple of minutes. Get up. Jump around. Scroll your social media feeds. Then plonk your ass in the chair and start the timer again.

Up the ante by keeping a spreadsheet of your sprints. I write down the date and the number of words I've written for each sprint (or the number of pages edited if I'm editing). I can see a visual record of a book's progress and whether I'm slacking off.

Before I started sprinting, I had no idea what my average word count per hour was. I suspect it was something like 500 words, possibly even less as I let social media and articles about writing distract me. Now I use sprinting, and I get between 700-1200 words per sprint. I try to write 4k words per day – 2k in the morning, 2k in the afternoon. (Bear in mind I have no day job!) With sprinting I'm able to get my words done in a couple of hours, leaving me with more time in the day to work on my business (and watch cat videos on YouTube).

The reason sprinting works is because of brain chemistry. The timer tricks your brain into feeling a sense of urgency. When we have an endless amount of time stretching out before us and a huge project to complete, it's easy to get distracted and tell ourselves we have time to do things later.

Even though I got good grades during high school and college, I was a classic procrastinator. I'd stare at an empty screen for hours, trying to conjure an essay from thin air. As soon as my deadline approached and things got hairy, I'd be able to pull out something amazing. Using sprinting I'm able to recreate this productivity without actually butting up too close for comfort with my deadlines.

You can even sprint together with other writers and gamify your writing even more. A lot of writers use programs like MyWriteClub or 4TheWords to set up a sprinting 'room' and invite other writers to join the fun.

I've found sprinting useful in my career, and perhaps you will, too.

FIND THE BEST TIME FOR YOU TO WRITE

There's a mantra you'll hear often: 'Writers write every day.' It's… sometimes true, often not.

For many writers, myself included, writing every day is how we create good habits and improve our craft. For me, writing is a great joy and I look forward to sitting down to get my words out. Even when I had a day job, the time I carved out for my writing was often the highlight of my day.

But not all writers work like this. Some people find tying writing down into a specific time slot saps the joy from the creative process. I know several writers who produce 3-6 books per year while writing nothing for whole periods, then locking themselves in a room or writers' retreat and blasting through the entire book in a few days or weeks.

All that time when they're not writing, they're still working. They're percolating on the characters and story. They might jot notes down about scenes or plot twists. They're reading and researching. But the actual words come out in a giant burst of uninterrupted productivity.

Similarly, some writers will do their best creative work early in the morning, before their household wakes up. Others like to wait for the dead of night, and others still are struck with late-afternoon inspiration. You need to try different times to figure out when you're at your best.

I'm not going to tell you to 'write every day.' What I am going to say is that you should experiment with different techniques, times and methods and find out what works for you and what brings you the most joy.

KNOW WHAT YOU'RE GOING TO WRITE

Some people need to be prepared before they start writing. They need to know what happens and where the book is heading before they can put the words down. If you sit down and stare at a blank page, it's probably because you feel unprepared. You may be trying to do the hardest work (figuring out what happens next) in the most time-consuming way (while you're knee-deep in a scene). Working all the details out first *may* be the way you improve your speed. It certainly works for many writers.

However, you may be like me – you don't want an outline. I use a technique I call Skeleton Drafting (I even have a mini-course on Skeleton Drafting if you think it could work for you - go to https://www.rageagainstthemanuscript.com/skeleton draftcourse to find out more).

For a skeleton draft, I know a few basic things before I start writing. I have an idea of the protagonist's personality and desires. I have an overarching hook for the book and the world. I roughly know where I'm starting and how it's going to end, and I might have a couple of scenes in mind. I start writing a rough draft of the first scene and then ask myself "What logically would happen next, knowing the main character's personality traits and the expectations of my genre?" I ask that question again and again as I continue to roughly draft the book until I get to the end.

A skeleton draft is rough – scenes may be only a few lines of dialogue or action, and I may not fully understand how they link together yet. When I'm finished with it, I have a 10-20k draft of what will become a 100k novel, and I understand the character's journey and more about who they are, and I'm ready to start from the beginning and flesh out the draft.

To write, I need to be in the character's head. If I create a detailed outline, I won't write the book. I know the story, so what's the point? It's not fun anymore. So I use the skeleton draft instead.

I recommend trying skeleton drafting, but if that's not for you, there's a great book I recommend you read. It's by an amazing historical fiction author named Libbie Hawker (she who writes in several different historical periods, mentioned in the pen names chapter) and it's called *Take Off Your Pants*. You'll also probably get a lot out of James Scott Bell's *Writing From the Middle*.

If you think you might be more of a plotter, I highly recommend several books. The Hero's Journey model was designed by Joseph Campbell. Randy Ingermanson's Snowflake Method. Francesca Lia Block's part-memoir, part-writing-instructive, *The Thorn Necklace*. Jessica Brody's screenwriting technique *Save the Cat! Writes a Novel*. Lisa Cron's *Story Genius*. K. M. Weiland's *Structuring Your Novel*.

Most writers sit somewhere along a spectrum between loving the extreme outline and starting with nothing. Try different outlining methods and see if it helps you. Cobble together aspects from different systems to create your own method. Go with what works for *you*.

BE KIND TO YOURSELF

You don't want to burn out on writing. Remember the core principle through which you should operate – it has to be fun. If you're not having fun and you're forcing yourself to write, that pain will be reflected in your words. If you're going through the motions, your readers will be able to tell, and you won't get any closer to your dreams.

Even though I've been super driven with my writing, 15+ years of working every spare moment when I wasn't at my day job have taken their toll from time to time. I thought I'd tell you a little cautionary tale about quitting my day job. OK, so I lied. It's not 'little.' Buckle up, cuz this is gonna take a while.

You already know that in Feb 2018 I got to do the super amazing incredible thing and quit my job as a copywriter at a tech startup to be a full-time author. What you might not know is that this isn't the first time I 'quit the day job' to be a writer. I did it in 2013. But less than six months later I was back in a salaried job.

I used to work as a braille transcriber. It was a wonderful job with great people that I enjoyed, but ever since I'd got out of university and realized I couldn't be an archaeologist, I'd been working toward this dream of writing full-time. I wanted to write novels and tell stories, but that was a long process involving submitting to editors and agents with no guarantees. I was young and impatient. I wanted it to happen NOW.

I think I've probably always been the type of person who really should be my own boss, and I was super keen to do that as soon as possible. I have been dreaming about quitting all my jobs basically ever since I started them. That's no reflection of the work I did, which was wonderful and rewarding, or the people I worked for, who were all lovely, but the fact that I didn't want to work with people. I find all the 'office stuff' – meetings, commuting, small talk, team-building, filing, just urgh, *all of it* – distracted from work. I liked the people I worked with, but with only a couple of exceptions, they weren't my friends, and I found it hard to pretend otherwise.

I started spending a lot of time taking on freelance work for other small business owners because I liked their vibe and I thought if I could make enough money doing that, I'd be able to buy myself more time to write fiction. I would get home from my day job and work until bedtime on client websites or tinkering with my novels.

After a few years, I had more freelance work than hours in

the day, and I still had to do my normal job and fit in fiction writing and normal people life stuff. I was getting seriously burned out working all the time. I was pulling in enough money for the hours I was putting in that my husband and I decided we'd take the chance and I'd quit my job and write full-time. At first, I stepped down to three days a week at my day job, then I built up the courage (and that was a lot of building) to go fully freelance.

I could work from home! I could set my own hours and be my own boss! I could have more free time for writing fiction! I was living the dream!

Hahahaha.

Turns out, I hated it. I was MISERABLE.

I worked more than ever. I could never switch off. I felt this incredible pressure to earn a certain amount of money to prove I could do it (this didn't come from my husband or other people – it came from me). I felt like if I wasn't working then I was wasting time.

I hadn't gotten used to the idea that a business owner's to-do list ever ends. I'd keep thinking, "I'll write these three articles and then I'll work on my book." But after those three articles, there would always be three more, and three more after that. I felt trapped. The timing was bad because we'd started to build our dream home. Money was tight, and I felt that if the whole thing fell apart it would be my fault.

I resented working to help other people achieve their creative dreams while mine sat on the back burner. I resented clients who argued, who refused to pay their invoices, who wanted more more more for less money (and I was already way undercharging, which was also another issue).

I had no time for my fiction because the pressure I put on myself to get client work done was too great. When I *did* sit down to write fiction, the words wouldn't come. I didn't have anything left for myself.

I cried because an editor I'd been working with for years

left and a deal that would see my books published fell through. I cried because it felt like all my hard work was for nothing.

I hated it so much that after six months, when one of my clients begged me to take a full-time job as a copywriter at their company, offering me over 50% more than what I had earned at my last position as a starting salary and said I could work three days a week from home, I took the job happily.

I felt like a failure. But I was determined that I'd learn from my mistakes. I wasn't going to repeat this.

When I took the job, I quit every one of my freelance clients. I accepted that running a service business wasn't where my passion or skills lie.

I declared that when my work hours were done, I would STOP WORKING. I was a good worker for the 40 hours I was at the job, but I never put in unpaid overtime even though it might have cost me some promotions. I was done giving all my creative energy to other people. I loved the 'think fast and break things' mentality of tech and the idea that shipping product is better than waiting until it's 100% perfect (I've probably carried a lot of that over into my own business), but I didn't love the mentality that the company was your life. I didn't want to use all my creative energy to make someone else rich.

(Also, there are only so many ways to make accounting software and vinyl siding interesting.)

(OK, not many ways at all).

I spent my free time working on my books. I learned about self-publishing. I dedicated myself to being a successful indie, but ONLY if I was having fun doing it.

I decided that I didn't have the fortitude to start a business and build a house at the same time. So I set myself a rule that I'd wait until the house was finished before I considered quitting again.

I taught myself to be grateful to my day job for giving me

the money to pay the mortgage while I learned and grew my readership and dealt with the stress of building.

I (tried to) stop beating myself up and calling myself a failure, because it wasn't true.

I (tried to) create better balance in my life. It worked. For a while. And then the old burnout crept back.

I was able to work from home three days a week at my first two positions, but because I'm blind and can't drive myself, my commute was 1:45 each way at one job and 1:30 each way at the next. I had to leave at a certain time to get a bus to my husband's office so we could drive home together. Sometimes when you are disabled riding public transport can be stressful – people can be rude and things go wrong and you don't know what's happened. It seemed dumb to do that stress and commute just to sit in the office with my headphones jammed in my ears because everyone talking around me was a distraction.

In 2017 I was at a marketing agency, and the company imploded. They lost their breadwinner client, and I came to work one day and discovered our team of eight was now a team of three. My husband and I were halfway through building a house. I'd just released a book that was a complete flop. I felt afraid for my financial security.

My husband thought it was the ideal time to quit, but I worried things would end up like last time. I also felt like staying at the agency was a bad idea. I was stressing about it. I hated the work. I hated the not-knowing. So I decided to leave. Maybe I'd look for something else. Maybe I'd write. I wasn't 100% sure.

The week I handed in my notice, my old boss from my first tech job called me. "Are you happy where you are?" he asked. "Because I've just become the marketing manager at a startup, and I have to build a team…"

I liked this guy. He was hard work, but I knew how to handle him. He challenged me constantly and understood my work-from-home needs and introverted ways, which I appreciated. I went to talk to the company CEO, and we got along well. I asked for an insane amount of money and they said yes.

There was a catch. Part of the culture of the company wanted everyone in the office, eating lunch together, brainstorming, etc. They wanted me to come in every day. I said two days. They said four days. It was 1:45 mins each way from my house.

My husband and I discussed it. We knew the next year was going to be what we needed to finish the house. We knew this job would mean a lot of extra work for me. It would be stressful, but I'd done stressful before and survived. "It's your call," he said. "But I think if you do it, you should put an end date on it. In a year, you leave and you write full-time."

So I said yes. And there began the most stressful year of my life.

The day before I started at work, my boss emailed me: "Oh, by the way, our office moved to a new suburb. Hope that's okay." The new suburb meant my commute now included a car ride and TWO buses and was 2:30 each way – 5 hours round-trip commuting and I had to leave work early to get to my husband, so I'd have to make up time when I got home.

I went in four days a week and had a bit of a meltdown after a month where I cried in a meeting because I was so tired and my back hurt (I was working hunched over a computer on the bus and in the car so I didn't have to work when I got home). Begrudgingly, they allowed me to drop down to three days a week in the office.

I wrote my quitting date in my calendar.

I did the math on the minimum I had to earn each month so we could pay the mortgage and keep our cats fed. I was about halfway to that number with my fiction. I knew I'd have to either have a hit book OR make up the rest with free-lance work.

I didn't want to count on a hit, so I put up a Facebook status saying I was looking for freelance work. I knew what I wanted – to work through an agency. They'd handle the clients, I'd just write things, which was the easy part for me. I ended up with work through a friend's brother, and he referred me to another agency, and before I knew it I had four small marketing studios giving me work. I was prepping to quit. The only thing was, it was only March/April – the house *still* wasn't finished, and I had to do this freelance work alongside my demanding copy job. AND writing my own books.

Here we go again.

I worked non-stop, basically from the moment I got up until I went to bed. I had my computer in front of me every night while we watched TV. I gave up weekend plans to work. I was doing two full-time jobs. The difference was that this time, I had an end date.

We poured the extra money into finishing the house and building some savings. We were getting closer to our goal, to the life we wanted.

This year strained my marriage like nothing else. We were stressed about the house. Even in the moments when my husband and I hung out, I wasn't present. I accepted too many invitations to go away to hike, to see friends, to teach writing and officiate weddings for extra money, just to get away from my computer. He felt as though I was getting away from him.

But… we had that end-date. Gods, how I looked to that end date with so much hope.

I didn't have a hit that year. In fact, my writing income dipped for the first six months. My dream looked further away than ever. But then I had my first BookBub (more on this later), and things picked up.

STEFF GREEN

I had so little time to work on my fiction that I focused only on the thing that made the most money – I wrote books. I didn't update Facebook or my blog or do pretty much any marketing apart from applying for BookBubs and sending out a newsletter when I published.

By the time November rolled around, I'd put on weight and I felt on the verge of crying ALL THE TIME. My brain turned to mush and the whole world felt sort of far away, like I was listening through water. I knew I was probably close to having a breakdown. I felt like I couldn't talk to people about it because I had done this to myself. Anyone I talked to would have (rightfully so) said, "So just stop."

December rolled around, and I was so close, so close. I started reading whychoose books, and they were such a wonderful escape from the stress that I started to wonder if maybe I wanted to write one. An idea came to me. I wrote *The Castle of Earth and Embers* in a flurry of inspiration – churning out 2,000 words a day on my bus commute with my laptop balanced precariously on my knees.

The excitement over that book was probably what got me through those last couple of months.

I released it the same day I handed in my notice, and it instantly became my bestselling book. For the first month ever I hit my income goal solely from fiction. It felt like a fucking sign from the universe.

One year nearly to the day since I started at that job, on my birthday, I said goodbye to the 5-hour commute. I had my last doughnut morning tea with my workmates. I went home in a daze. I couldn't quite believe it.

Best birthday present ever.

On my first day as a full-time writer, I bounced out of bed at the crack of dawn. I wrote 5k words on *The Castle of Fire and Fable*. I cooked dinner and played with the cats. I ACTUALLY watched a movie with my husband. It was the best day in a very long time.

I spent 2018 writing the Briarwood series and focusing on growing my fiction income. I increased my financial goal, and one by one I dropped the agencies as clients as I got closer to that goal. I started to put long-term plans into action to ensure the business was sustainable.

I (mostly) stopped working in the evenings and week-ends. The house was done. My husband and I worked hard to communicate better and to enjoy the house and life we'd built. It was one of the BEST years of our marriage.

So that's my 'how I quit' story. It's also my 'do as I say, not as I do' story about being kind to yourself and not giving yourself a breakdown over writing, cuz it's not worth it. *(Except when it is)*.

Probably don't do what I did and work yourself toward burnout and hurt your marriage. But having the 'end-date' thing was a great idea, as was using more stable freelance work as a transition. Also, stash some money in the bank. We had a few months of mortgage payments as a buffer. Quitting wasn't a financial decision so much as a mental health one for me. I needed to make this happen. I needed to know if I could do it. And that was the best decision I ever made.

What I've tried to show you in this section is how you might be able to increase your output. You're going to have to do some experimenting and figure out what works for you. Gamifying your process with sprints might be awesome for you, or it might make you feel trapped. Getting away for a few days might help you smash out an entire novel, or you could spend the whole time staring blankly at the wall. Plotting out your book in detail with index cards and spreadsheets might help you get to grips with the story, or it could make you feel as though the whole exercise is pointless. We're all different and our brains respond in unique ways.

To me, it all comes back to my mantra of having fun. If a technique feels too much like hard work like you're trying to stifle your creativity, ditch it. Find what feels fun and effortless to you, and just do more of that.

Becca Syme is a lovely person and an author who has developed solid techniques for writing faster. Listen to an awesome interview she did on the SPA Girls podcast.

Rachel Aaron is another author who writes a lot about hacking her process. She went from writing 2k a day to 10k a day, and she's got an amazing book called – not surprisingly – *2k to 10k – Writing Faster, Writing Better, and Writing More of What You Love* – all about her process.

YOU ARE YOUR OWN PUBLISHING HOUSE

When you're writing and editing your book, you are a creative. You get to live inside your characters and do all the artsy thinking that makes writing so much fun.

However, at all other times, you need to put aside your writer's brain and engage your publisher's brain. I've already introduced you to my 'hat' analogy. Imagine yourself putting down your writer hat as soon as you write 'THE END' and picking up your publisher hat.

A publisher can still be creative, but they're also an astute business person. They know the market, they've done their research, and they can make strategic decisions that will drive their company forward.

For example, you-the-writer may have five different ideas for what you want to write next. That's the creative part. You-the-publisher will have to look at those ideas strategically and think about what's the best fit for your current backlist and what is likely to get you closer to your goals.

(If you-the-publisher is particularly savvy, you might be checking out the bestseller charts in your genre, looking at trends and covers, and thinking about how you could work your ideas to fit one of those trends).

You-the-publisher get the fun job of planning your

releases for any given year. Because you've only got one writer (you!) and finite resources, you'll only have so many release spots to fill. You have to think carefully about how best to use those spots.

After you-the-publisher have done your thing, you-the-marketer has the job of making sure as many readers as possible are aware of the books you release.

Switching between your three hats is a concept I will refer back to because I think it helps you to compartmentalize. If you've never run a business before, you will need to learn some new skills. That's cool – learning is interesting. And maybe you think that you won't be good at business, but a) I bet that's not true and b) remember that all sorts of people run successful businesses in vastly different ways. Just like there are no real rules in writing, there's no 'one rule of business,' and you get to decide what works for you.

As the publishing house, you get to decide the rules and set the release schedule. You can change things if they aren't working. You can crack the whip when you need to and give yourself a fucking break when things feel overwhelming. You're the boss, so be the kind of boss you've always wanted – fun, clever, and kind.

HOW TO ROCK WRITING FASTER:

- How fast do you write right now? Can you get some sense of the number of words you write in a day? This will give you a starting point.
- Put on your publishing hat and look strategically at your publishing schedule. Choose projects that are most likely to bring you closer to your goals.
- Set a schedule that's workable but just a *little* beyond your reach. If it's taken you a year to write your first book, you probably can't go straight into writing a book a month, but can you produce two

books this year? What about three? Four can't be that hard…

- Find a space to carve out 20 minutes per day to write. Enlist your family or roommates to help you keep on track.
- Sprint. Set the timer and go, go, go!
- If sprinting isn't for you, try binge-writing. Schedule a few days where you have no interruptions. Get out of the house if possible. Send the kids to their grandparents. Go, go, go!
- Try writing at different times of the day. Notice when writing feels joyful and flows freely. Notice when you struggle for every word.
- Read writing craft/outline books and try different techniques. Throw away what feels like work and keep anything that makes writing more fun.
- Track your progress in a notebook or spreadsheet. For each sprint, write down the number of words you write and a total for the day. Let your growing word count be a motivation!
- Get some writer accountability buddies. You might find a fellow writer on Rage Against The Manuscript to sprint with and share your triumphs!
- Be aware of the signs of burnout and fatigue. Make sure you have people in your life who will call you on your bullshit when you need them – because if you're anything like me, you'll forget to take care of yourself sometimes.

CHAPTER 5
MAKE READING ENJOYABLE

IF YOU WANT to keep readers coming back for more of your books, you need to give them a good reading experience. This means not springing nasty surprises on them that are outside their genre – for example, killing off the hero in a romance novel, or suddenly turning a cosy mystery into a horror story. It also means crafting the best story possible – free of typos and continuity or grammatical errors.

As the author, you can improve the enjoyment of your readers by:

a. Writing 'to market' and following genre conventions.
b. Using an editor/proofreader.
c. Using formatting to create an easy reading experience.
d. Only put out your best work.

Let's look at these one at a time.

WRITING WHAT YOUR READERS WANT

Being a writer means pouring your heart onto the page. But it also means acknowledging that writing involves two parties – the writer and the audience. The people who make a living writing or see success with their projects generally consider their audience at least as much as they consider their proclivities.

If you want readers to keep buying your books, you've got to give them what they want. What readers want is, "More of the same stuff I love with some fun twists."

We've talked a little about genre in previous chapters, especially about how genre informs the way readers search for books. Within each genre, there are certain unwritten 'rules.' Sometimes writers break those rules and are very successful, but those are usually writers who already have a big audience and who are strategically moving outside of conventions. They are the exceptions – I choose to believe I'm not going to be the exception.

Generally speaking, you need to follow the rules of your genre if you want to appeal to readers. Give them more of the same stories they love, just with a fresh twist.

In a detective story, the mystery is always unravelled at the end of the book. In a romance, the couple overcomes their obstacles and gets their happily ever after. In fantasy, good triumphs over evil. You should know the tropes and features of your genre because you should be reading in the genre you write in. TV Tropes is also a great site to look at for lists of common tropes, as is just searching online for common tropes in your genre. (Warning: TV Tropes is a rabbit hole of fascination and you will be lost for days).

We call this 'writing to market.' Authors will often talk about 'writing to trend' and 'writing to market.' These two things are common techniques authors use to find and grow their audience. They may sound like synonyms, but they refer to specific techniques:

WRITING TO TREND

This means spotting trends before they hit it big and being one of the earliest authors out with a trendy book. Trends swing in and out of favour with readers – what's hot one month may be gone the next. Many traditional publishers try to predict trends, but it's hard for them because they schedule books a year (or more) before they're published. As a self-published author, you can have a book to market in a month or less, so you can jump on an emerging trend.

You have to be fast to spot a trend before it gets big and get your book out because there are lots of authors (many with huge followings) doing the same thing. If you're too late on a trend, your book will be crushed by the competition.

There's a lot of potential money to be made if you get in early on a trend, but long-term it can hurt your business. If you're always jumping on the next big thing, you may not be building a cohesive author brand. You may also be stressing yourself out and relying on big hits.

The romance genre (where I write) has seen its share of trends over the years. A few years ago, it was stepbrother romances. Right now it is bully romance. Paranormal has historically been all about vampires, but for the last decade, it's been all-shifters-all-the-time. Then Academy books styled after Harry Potter were the big thing, then romantasy, and now vampires are coming back from the dead (hahaha).

What's next? Who knows?

WRITING TO MARKET

Writing to market means that instead of going off on what-ever weird thing YOU want to write, you create the types of stories your readers have already told you (with their buying habits) that they love. A to-market book may also be trendy, but they tend to be more evergreen because they focus on tried-and-true favourite reader tropes.

This doesn't mean you're 'selling out.' Don't let anyone tell you that! If you genuinely love your genre and your work, then there is nothing wrong with being smart about what you choose to write for whom. This is you wearing your publishing hat and using the information available to make the best business decisions.

Remember what I said right from the start? If you're not having fun in this business, then what are you doing here? There are much easier ways to make a living. But you can have a total blast writing to market. I think it's more fun because you end up with a bigger audience – and readers are seriously the coolest people. I want to hang out with them all the time.

Both writing to market and writing trends involve studying your genre and its readers. You've got to get to know them like they were your BFFs. Figure out what resonates in the stories they love, and give them more of THAT. It means keeping a close eye on the bestseller lists in your genre and which books readers are talking about. It means reading widely in your genre and identifying what works and doesn't work *for readers*. It means analyzing covers, blurbs and characters and collecting data to improve your craft and marketing.

The difference between writing to market and writing trends is that trend-writers take the lessons learned from writing to market and apply them to tropes, niches and subgenres that readers are gagging for RIGHT NOW. That trend may wane weeks or months from now, so they need to get on it while it's hot.

If you're writing to market, you may find that sometimes you are perfectly positioned to spot and react to trends. This happened to me with my Kings of Miskatonic Prep series. Because I was paying careful attention to the market and I'd worked hard to hone my process so that I could write fast, I was able to come up with an idea I knew my readers would love that spoke to an emerging trend, get the pre-order up ASAP, write the book in three weeks, and be one of the early books. It was an amazing stroke of luck that propelled that series to the top of the Amazon charts, but I don't count on hitting a successful trend with every release because I haven't built my strategy around chasing trends. I don't even write to market. I used to think I did, but it turns out…

WRITING TO VIBE

I wanted to add this third section because I feel like a complete imposter advising you to 'write to trend' or even 'write to market' when that's not what I do.

I've talked about this elsewhere in this book, but after the success of Kings of Mistakonic Prep, I spent two years writing very on-trend, on-market dark romance because I thought that's who I was as a writer. It turns out, that's not the case. Those dark romance books had solid sales, but I was never top of the genre or writing the kind of books everyone talked about.

I realised that I wasn't happy using this strategy. These weren't the kind of books I wanted to write forever, and I didn't want to write books that felt the same as everyone else's.

Becca Syme talks about this in some of her resources (you can check out Becca's work for writers at https://betterfaster academy.com/). Some authors are all about the fandom/world they've created. Some are superstars who draw readers because of who they are as a personality. Some regenerate their career every few years based on writing the kind of books that are selling, and some are experimenters who throw a lot of stuff out there and see what works.

I was writing solid, popular books that were selling right now, but I felt as though I wasn't creating any longevity for myself. My career felt precarious. And I wasn't happy, because I learned that's not the kind of author I am.

I wanted the kind of fans who create memes about a world, who cosplay as your characters, who buy merch and immerse themselves in your world. I didn't want to do what everyone else was doing. When people said the name 'Steffanie Holmes' I wanted them to immediately think of my unique books (and only mine).

So I pivoted to writing in the Nevermore Bookshop world again, and it was a smashing success. And the weird thing is, based on everything I've learned, it shouldn't have been. The Nevermore Bookshop series is not trendy. it's not 'to market.' It's not even a genre. But it worked because of vibes.

This is much harder to define than writing to market or writing to trends.

- Although Nevermore is not in a genre, it is adjacent to a lot of genres that have space – it's KIND OF cosy fantasy, paranormal romance, paranormal women's fiction, cosy mystery…it doesn't fit any of those genres, but it contains elements of them that call to readers – you will like this book.
- The books incorporate a set of 'vibes' that sum up the reading experience. These vibes can then be used as part of marketing your books. These vibes may include mixing tropes from different genres, nostalgic experiences, certain types of characters, and immersive sensory details that go together to create a vibe.
- Sensory immersion is important in these books, with lots of descriptions that evoke certain moods

and experiences, and additional details that might not add to the plot/character but provide a sensory experience – food, flowers, etc.

- Vibes books focus on character arcs over particularly clever and intricate plots.
- The vibes and characters create a sense of belonging. The reader feels as though they recognise themselves (or their ideal selves) in the stories.
- These stories also evoke strong aesthetic themes that authors can then use in their marketing. It's often the aesthetics that first attract readers to the books.
- The setting is often vitally important. The setting is another character in a vibe book and elicits a feeling of nostalgia, wonder, timeliness, or curiosity.
- Humorously self-aware. This might just be a 'me' thing, but I feel as though books and authors who do vibes tend to be quite self-aware and will mock themselves lightly in their books in a way that endears you to them. There is often a lot of humour in vibes books, even if they're dark.

Some authors who I think do this very well are Grady Hendrix, T Kingfisher, and CG Drews. Yes, those are all traditional authors. I don't see this so much in indie author circles because of everything discussed in this book (basically, advice for indies is largely about writing trends or writing to market and I do think, if you want to make a living at this, on the whole, it's good advice), but I think there's space for vibes books to be done well.

If you think you might fit into this category, here's my advice:

- Ask yourself if this is REALLY you, or if you are just looking for an excuse as to why your not-to-market books aren't selling.
- Vibes books tend to be JUST SLIGHTLY OFF the market, but they can still be placed beside some other popular books. A reader can say, "If I liked these books, I'll like THIS book" even if the book includes elements that are outside their normal reader. This is something you can use for your marketing – showcasing other popular books alongside yours as a way to explain the vibes.
- Vibes books tend to have a very relatable, slightly quirky main character, the kind of character a reader can easily imprint themselves upon.
- When writing, narrow in on how you want the reader to feel – use setting, descriptions, and little details to evoke that feeling.
- Books with strong vibes might also be a more straight-up genre mash or mash of two popular tropes.
- Think about the aesthetics, activities, moods, foods, smells, and characters that go with your vibes. Make a big list of 100 words that fit your book's vibes. Use these in your book marketing as jumping-off points for content, and to create lists and memes around your book's vibes.
- Nostalgia is also a touchstone in vibes books. Using memes from pop culture or a certain era can help get across the vibes you're creating.
- Some vibes are just more appealing than others. Writing to vibes is NOT THE EASY ROUTE, and you may perfectly nail the vibes in your books only to find that those vibes don't resonate with readers.
- Artwork, special editions, aesthetics will help vibes writers more than any other type of writer.

Writing to vibes has been a big part of what made my career, so I believe it's a viable, if somewhat loopy, path to success in self-publishing. But you have to be prepared that your books may not hit as high as writers who focus on a specific genre or trend. But if your vibes are right, there's a sustainable indie career for you.

BETA-READERS, EDITORS, AND PROOFREADERS

Have at least one person *who is not you* read over your work. Ideally, you should hire a professional editor and/or proof-reader to ensure you're giving readers a quality book. Some editors and proofreaders specialize in working with indies, and they are affordable. I pay around $400 USD for my editor for an 80,000-word manuscript.

If that's too much for you right now, you may be able to swap services with another author or editor or bribe a friend or family member who's great at grammar to take a look. Even using free programs like Grammarly or having your computer read your manuscript aloud will help you spot mistakes and clunky sentences.

There are lots of different types of useful people writers use. You'll see other writers talking about their:

- **Beta-reader:** Someone who casts a critical eye over your manuscript before it goes to any other editor. Usually, betas aren't professional editors, but they are voracious readers. Instead of picking up typos, they focus on story stuff – are they excited during this chapter? Does the protagonist resonate? Is someone acting out of character? Do they notice continuity or plot errors? Incorporating their feedback can help make your story more engaging and fix wider issues. Many of my friends send their betas each chapter as they complete it. This freaks me out! I have one beta – my husband – and I give him the manuscript as soon as I've finished. He has two weeks to give me feedback.

- **Developmental editor:** Kind of a professional version of a beta reader. Your developmental editor will give you feedback on your style, plot, characters, and the big picture of your book. Many people recommend developmental editors as you're learning to write a novel. I never used one until last year, when I decided that part of my strategy was improving the things I'm already good at, like writing. I found the developmental editor more useful now that I'm at a higher level than I would have if I'd used her as an inexperienced author. I think her feedback is a big part of why the book she worked on was picked up for a trad deal. So don't discount the value of a developmental editor even if you know how to write a good book.
- **Editor/line editor/copy editor:** Different people call this stage different things. I just call it 'editing,' and I work with a professional who goes over my manuscript like a boss. She picks up spelling and grammar my Grammarly pass missed, but also style issues like repetitive prose and continuity, and offers suggestions to improve tension or syntax, word choice, and strength of prose.
- **Proofreader:** A final pass to pick up stray typos and grammar issues. Your proofreader is the last person to see the manuscript. I skip this stage and find that my ARC readers will pick up most of the remaining stray typos.

No law says you need all four of them, or any of them. It's up to you to find a process that works for you. For most of my career, I've put my manuscript through Grammarly to catch the most glaring errors, then I use a beta reader (the afore-mentioned cantankerous drummer husband) and a professional editor. Sometimes a proofreader, but I've found this less essential as I've improved my craft and process.

Since my last book, a developmental editor has been part of my process, before the book goes to my husband.

Even with professional editors, mistakes creep through or you introduce your own errors, and it's okay!

Let me tell you a mortifying story. On my July 2017 release, I had a minor character named Rita. My editor suggested her name was too close to my main character's name, Rosa. I went to my manuscript and did a find/replace all on Rita's name with a substitute – Margaret. Problem solved. I launched the book. It sold around 3,500 copies before a reader emailed me to tell me that three times in the book I had the word hemargaretge, and was this possibly a spelling error? It turns out that when I did that find/replace I'd also changed the word 'heritage' to 'hemargaretge' and NO ONE had pointed it out.

Once I stopped feeling sick, I was able to laugh about it.

The moral of the story is to remind you to be VERY careful with find/replace, especially on your final manuscript. But also, to tell you that readers don't need your book to be *perfect*. They want a good story. If you have too many errors it will impact their ability to read, and that will annoy them – and they'll tell you in reviews. However, if you tell a good yarn and you've got a few spelling mistakes, they'll still consider you a favourite author.

I try to always think of my writing as a business (because it is). Don't bring an inferior product to market. Get the best editing and cover you can within your budget. Find a process that works for you. But don't spend years fiddling and proofing the book as an excuse to not publish it – no matter how many times you read through, you'll still miss mistakes and you'll still want to tweak the prose. At some point, you've got to take the plunge and hit publish.

FORMATTING

Formatting your work for publishing means creating a lovely document that your reader's device can understand. Their device will then present your work in the best possible way and enable them to view images, click on links, see bold and italics, and use a table of contents to jump around the book.

First I'm going to talk about ebook formatting. The reason for this is that if you whip your file into shape for an ebook, you can use that same file to create a paperback in less time, but it will be a bit harder the other way around. Your formatted file will also be useful to give to your audiobook narrator.

The word processing program you use to write your work will give you a certain file type – usually a doc, docx, or txt. This file may look nice and tidy to you on your computer screen, but what matters is the code going on in the background. When the file is converted to the e-reader format (MOBI or EPUB), the computer has to be given the correct signals so it knows when a chapter begins, when a word is bolded, and when there's a link in the text.

You can upload a docx file as is to Amazon and it will create an ebook. However, that ebook won't be a joy to read. People won't be able to navigate through the chapters. It might have random sections in a different font. Tables and bulleted lists will probably be a total mess. This is because what you see on your screen isn't the same as what appears on an e-reader. The words will be the same, but if you haven't used the right formatting language, the e-reader won't know where a chapter begins or why a text has five hard returns.

You want readers to be able to navigate the file – skip to a chapter they want to read, see headings and subheadings, notice quotations by indenting them, etc. Putting in these features during the word processing stage has to be done in a certain way if you want them to carry through the conversion process.

A properly formatted file is also a huge benefit to anyone with a print disability (for example, visually impaired or blind readers like me) as it will enable their screen reader to pick up on formatting.

HOW TO FORMAT YOUR EBOOK FILE

Start with a file that's as 'clean' as possible. If you use 'styles' in MS Word, Google Docs, etc, then you'll be ensuring your file is free from strange formatting that will cause problems during conversion. You'll also be creating a file that can be navigated.

The first thing you do before you try any formatting is to select all the text in your file and click 'normal style.' This will delete any back-end code you've accidentally added during the writing process and give you that 'clean' file while retaining style elements like italics. Now, go through the file and add headings, and bulleted lists using styles, links, and page breaks (never hit the 'return' key multiple times to break a page – always use 'insert > page break').

Using styles means that if you have a chapter heading 'chapter 1', instead of highlighting those words and choosing a font and a text size and centring them on the page, you highlight and select 'heading 1' from the styles/formatting dropdown menu. Use 'heading 1' for all chapter headings, 'heading 2' for all subheadings, and 'blockquotes' for any quoted text.

You can now create a table of contents by writing out a list of chapter headings and then linking each one within your file to the corresponding chapter heading. Add front matter (copyright page, an epigraph, dedication) and back matter (about the author, other books by the author, excerpt or blurb for a future book in the series, link to sign up to your newsletter, etc) separating each element with a page break.

This is how you manually format a file. Most authors don't do this – it will generate a perfectly readable but generic-looking ebook file, and it will take you time to learn and perfect. (especially the table of contents. OMG. NEVER AGAIN).

I use Vellum – a formatting software suite that creates beautiful ebooks and print books in no time at all. Vellum has been hands down one of the best investments I've ever made in my business.

Currently, Vellum is Mac-only, but many PC users run it by using a service called MacinCloud. There is another popular formatting suite called Atticus that will work on a PC. I haven't used it, so I can't comment. But I've read plenty of books formatted in Atticus and I'd say they're just as pretty and easy-to-use as Vellum-formatted books!

There are other ways to get your formatting done. Some writers use a program called Calibre. The Draft2Digital distributor offers a free formatting tool for ebook and print, and Amazon has Kindle Create, which is a free Kindle-only formatting tool.

You could also outsource your formatting to another company. If you're only writing a single book or you find the concepts above a real headache, then this might be a good option for you. I feel that formatting is so easy to learn that if you're planning on publishing more than one book (see guideline 2), I DIY it to save on production costs. Doing it yourself means you can quickly make changes to an ebook or print file without having to pay extra or wait in a work queue.

You may think you won't make changes to an ebook once you publish it, but take it from someone who frequently updates her ebooks to edit typos, change backmatter, and add maps – you will. YOU WILL.

Note on images: You can use images in your ebook file, but beware. Kindle adds a 'delivery fee' to cover the cost of sending your file to a Kindle. The larger your formatted file, the higher this delivery fee. If you use tons of large images, your delivery fee might get so high it eats significantly into your royalty. If possible, cut back images in the ebook to only the essentials, or use the Kindle Kids' Book Creator, Kindle Comic Creator, or Kindle Textbook Creator, which are all specifically designed for books with tons of images.

You might like to cut some images and include them instead as bonus content for a newsletter signup or on your website, or save them for social media sharing.

Once you have this clean file for your ebook, you can import it into a print template to create your print formatting. Both KDP Print and IngramSpark offer print templates in a variety of sizes, which will help you make sense of common print issues like widow/orphans and page numbering. Or, like me, you could use Vellum. Sweet, sweet headache-saving Vellum.

PRODUCING YOUR BEST WORK

My last point, and I think this goes without saying for you, but I'm gonna say it anyway, is not to just churn out any old guff because you think it will sell. Respect your readers. Give them a book you care about, and they'll care about it, too.

PIRACY AND DRM

Any time I run a self-publishing workshop, I'm asked about DRM and about how to stop people from pirating my book. My answer is, "I don't care."

Why? The majority of readers are wonderful people who are perfectly happy to pay for a book to be sent directly to their device. Those are the readers I write for, and I want to make it as easy as possible for them to enjoy my books across all their devices. DRM makes it harder for them to access my books, and it makes life especially difficult for blind and low-vision readers (of which I am one).

Piracy will happen whatever I do. If I scour the internet for illegal downloads of my books and send DMCA take-down notices, the books will be back up in a few days. If I use DRM on my books, a skilled pirate can break it in minutes. I choose to accept that piracy comes hand-in-hand with building an audience, and so I let it go on as long as it doesn't impact my career.

I came into the heavy metal music scene during the age of Kazaa. Before that, I used to tape my favourite songs off the radio. I'm aware of how piracy can be a catalyst for a band's success, as people pass the music around. Although I would profoundly prefer readers buy my books, if someone falls in love with my characters from a pirated novel and becomes a lifelong fan, *at some point* I am going to make some money off them. They'll buy a $100 special edition or they'll buy a ticket to an event or they'll tell ten friends to read my book and those ten friends read my book in KU. As long as the piracy isn't impacting my career, I'm mostly happy to let it go and not worry about it.

When piracy becomes an issue is when it *does* affect your career. Sometimes, people who pirate your books will try to make money off them by putting them up for sale.

I've heard of authors who have run afoul of Amazon's algorithms because pirated books up for sale on iBooks or Nook are technically breaking KU's exclusivity clauses. Usually, showing Amazon that you've sent a takedown notice and that those books are up on known pirate sites will get them off your back, but as you may come to discover, dealing with Amazon will yield different results depending on who you talk to, the day of the week, the phase of the moon, and how many goats you sacrifice.

(No goats were harmed in the publishing of this book).

If I see piracy of my books (readers usually point them out), I'll send out the notices, but I don't actively go out looking for it.

AI is making piracy more prevalent because an AI can take a book and sliiiiightly rewrite it so Amazon's bots don't catch it. These books aren't going to be very good, but they are out there, being annoying.

Another form of piracy I see quite often is people putting audiobooks up for free listening on YouTube. The pirate then makes money from the ads that run during your audiobook. Youtube has a fast takedown system – I've used this numerous times.

There are companies you can hire who send out takedown notices and look for these types of books. My friends find them effective. Or just adopt an, "I don't care until I do attitude" like me.

HOW TO MAKE YOUR BOOKS A JOY TO READ:

- Figure out what budget you have available for producing your book. For your first book, you have four main potential costs: cover, editing, formatting, and marketing. If you need to prioritize where to spend money, make cover/editing number one.
- Study your market/genre/niche/vibes. You might like to create spreadsheets and list titles with your observations, or you could just look through the bestseller lists and take note of what you see. You should be reading books in your genre so you know what readers are craving.
- Figure out five things readers crave that you can include in your novel – tropes, character types, cover elements, etc. Are you hitting the beats that make readers come back for more?

- Look for beta readers or an editor. Ask around in your friend/family circles, or talk to other writers for their recommendations. Most service providers will edit a few pages for free as a sample. It may take you a few tries to find someone you click with, but once you do it'll be like finding the perfect hairdresser – you'll never let them go.

- Be open to criticism. This is harder than it sounds, and it may take you time to work through the resistance of hearing people critique your work. Difficult, but essential to improving as a writer. Remember, if you surround yourself with the right people, they are never critiquing you as a person, only what you've created, and only because they want to help you make it the best it can be.

- Try formatting your ebook file from scratch, just to see how you do. The more you can use styles and clean formatting, the better you'll find your formatting experience whether you DIY or use a tool like Vellum. You'll find plenty of follow-along tutorials on YouTube if you're feeling confused.

- Ask yourself, "Am I proud of this book?" and "Am I having fun?" If the answer is yes, then it doesn't matter what happens when you publish or what other people say about you, you've done an awesome thing!

CHAPTER 6
COVER. TITLE. BLURB: THEY MATTER

AS AN INDIE AUTHOR without direct distribution into bookstores, you're probably going to make most of your sales online as digital ebooks.

As you learned in the first chapter, research from Author Earnings has shown that 65% of readers now prefer digital devices for fiction. Tiktok and special editions have made print trendy again, which is super cool. Also, other markets (non-fiction, children's books, etc) are growing, too. Certain genres will always have a huge print market – coffee table books, children's picture books, literary fiction, etc – and it's important as an author and publisher to understand how people in your genre are reading your books. It will likely be digitally.

We're going to deal with direct sales of physical books in a later section. But everything in this chapter about cover, title, and blurb is vital whether you're selling digital or high-end special edition hardcovers.

Even if you're not a digital reader yourself, you need to find ways to reach those readers. And that means understanding how they search for and choose books.

YOUR TITLE

For most of us, the title of your book will appear during the writing process. I usually have my title in place before I even start writing. For fiction, your title should speak to the genre you're writing and evoke something of the mood, setting, and character of the book. Fun books might employ puns and other word tricks to alert readers to the character's voice. Darker books will use emotive language to evoke mood and setting. Objects and names can be used to create a certain look and feel. If you have a unique plot element, character trait, or setting, you might like to pick out this fact using the title.

Look at how other authors in your genre title their work. Without copying, can you use the same patterns and language to convey to readers that they might enjoy your book? Experiment with different words and lengths until you come up with something you like. If you can't choose between different titles, test them out on readers or fellow writers you trust.

For non-fiction, your title needs to clearly state the purpose of the book and what the reader will learn. It's also great if it can convey something of the book's style and tone so the reader knows what type of experience they can expect. For example, this book – *Rage Against the Manuscript: Your Guide to Rocking Self-Publishing, Finding Your Readers, and Building a Killer Author Brand* – tells you exactly what you're going to learn about (self-publishing) while also letting you know it's gonna be served up with a bit of my punk/metal ethos.

You also want your non-fiction title to elicit an emotional response. Your readers have a specific problem – they pick up your book because they believe you have a solution. Beware of a title that repeats their problem back to them. This will give an emotional response, all right – one of fear and resentment. E.g., *Got Some Enemies At Your Gates And You Don't Know What To Do With Them.*

Instead, focus on how your book will solve the problem for them, and how they will learn new skills to reach their desired end-state. *The Practical Guide for Building Your Own Medieval Siege Engine, Protecting Your Castle, and Conquering Your Neighbours.*

For individual titles in a series, consider following a pattern. All my series have a distinct pattern that makes it clear the books belong together. For example, my Briarwood Witches series has five books as follows:

> The Castle of Earth and Embers
> The Castle of Fire and Fable
> The Castle of Water and Woe
> The Castle of Wind and Whispers
> The Castle of Spirit and Sorrow

And my Kings of Miskatonic Prep series all have one-word titles in the past tense:

> Shunned
> Initiated
> Possessed
> Ignited

You might like to enlist your readers to help you come up with titles, especially for future books in a series. My Nevermore Bookshop Mysteries series titles all include murderous puns of famous book titles or bookish phrases. I had a few ideas in place for the series when I enlisted the help of my readers. They came up with some AMAZING ideas. Even though the series is now complete with ten books, I have six more amazing titles saved up in case I get the chance to write more in the future.

If you're writing a series, you'll also need a series title. Again, look for themes and elements important to the story that stretch across all four books. Most importantly, your series title should convey your genre. You can be overt about this and use keywords in your series title. For example, cosy mystery writer H. Y. Hanna has the Bewitched by Chocolate Mysteries (paranormal witchy mystery series set in a chocolate shop) and the English Cottage Garden Mysteries (murder mysteries focused around an English cottage garden/nursery). Fans of the genre can tell just from the series title if the books involve elements they enjoy.

Dark romance books set in high school or college will usually have the school's name in their series title, as this gives a clue to the setting and expected tropes. Crime novels will over have the main detective's name as the series title, which tells the reader what kind of story they can expect.

Speak your title aloud. Does it roll off your tongue? Is it easy to remember and repeat? You want people to recall your title so they can tell their friends all about it.

Once you've come up with a book/series title, it's probably worthwhile searching it on Amazon to see what other books have been published with the same title. You can still use a title if another author has used it (unless it's trademarked or you live in a country like Germany where this is illegal), but you don't want readers to get confused, so I'd avoid this if the other title is a similar genre.

YOUR BOOK COVER

People browsing online first see your book's cover in thumbnail form, so it needs to be bold and eye-catching. Your cover needs to look similar to other covers in your genre (so readers can find what they want to read) but also stand out because of its beautiful design and bold title. This sounds hard to achieve, and it is. That's why it's best to hire a specialist book cover designer to create an amazing cover for you. There are plenty of designers who specialize in book covers for indie authors, and they're relatively affordable. I pay between $150–500 for my book covers.

If that's unaffordable for you right now, consider a premade cover. Many cover designers will offer a selection of 'premade' or template cover designs for $30-70. You choose one that suits your book and genre, and the designer will exchange the placeholder text with your author's name and book title. You won't be able to make other changes to the cover, but you'll have a professional design ready to rock. You could always upgrade your books with new covers later if they do well.

Some authors are using AI to create their covers. I'm not personally a big fan of this for numerous reasons. I'd rather pay a human artist to create something awesome. But we're talking about your career, not mine. I want to give you all the options. If you want to go the AI route, remember that as of the date of this book's publication, AI words cannot be copyrighted.

Remember how we spoke about your author branding? This should be present on your covers. A reader should be able to look at one of your books and instantly recognize it as yours. Most authors do this by keeping the same font and placement for their name, and by ensuring their name is large and bold so it can be seen in thumbnail. You might choose the same colours and/or the same style of cover across multiple books/series to further solidify your branding.

Series branding is also important. Books in the same series should retain a similar look/feel/colour scheme/font throughout. When you hire your cover designer, make sure they know how many books are in the series so they can choose a cover model with multiple poses. Look for premade series book covers – if you find a cover you like but it's only a single, ask the designer if they'd be able to create it into a series.

OTHER TIPS FOR BOOK COVERS

Think like a reader. As a writer, you may be tempted to choose the most unusual and visually impactful design. If it doesn't look like other books in the genre then readers won't be able to identify your book as something they'd enjoy.

Likewise, leave behind fancy scrollwork lettering and tiny fonts – your title and name need to be big and bold so they can be read in thumbnail size. (A little bit of scrollwork is totally fine, though…if it suits your genre).

Stay on top of genre trends. If you use cover elements that were big 10-20 years ago, you risk having your books look old and tired. Browse the top 100 book lists in your genre on Amazon and other platforms to see what's selling in your genre *now.*

(SOMETIMES it can be a clever idea to buck this and use nostalgia to sell your books. Katee Robert did this with her Deal with a Demon series, where she had classic, Mills & Boon-style clinch covers made for a monster romance series. Readers devoured these faster than a blue alien with a mail-order bride. Nostalgia can sell, especially with a fun twist. This is something I'm considering for special edition books in the future.)

Beware of cover designers setting trends. Some authors like to hang out in cover designer groups and use the premade covers designers put up as research into what authors are writing now for release in 2-3 months. This sounds like a great idea in theory, but be wary. A couple of years back we saw *mermaidpalooza* – every paranormal and fantasy cover designer was making mermaid book covers.

Many predicted mermaid was a growing trend, but this wasn't reflected in the bestseller lists or the number of mermaid books hitting the shelves. It was simply cover designers being inspired by each other and having fun.

Give good instructions to your designer. Your designer can only go off the information you provide them. Every designer I've used has a questionnaire I fill in for each book/series, outlining what the book is about and the mood/feeling I want for the cover.

Pick out key elements of the story the designer can highlight on the cover – for example, for my Kings of Miskatonic Prep series, I gave my designer a list of objects that had some symbolic meaning in the series: theatre mask, book, tiara, skull, candle, artist palette, occult items, knife, diploma, etc. She chose some of these elements to use as the focal point on the covers.

If you need models on the cover, provide details like hair and eye colour, and the amount of flexibility you have with these. It's really helpful to provide examples of other covers in your genre you like. It's even more useful to explain in a sentence or two what you like/don't like about those covers.

Test covers. If you can't figure out which direction to go with a cover, have two options made and use a Facebook ad on your pre-order page to test which cover gets the most clicks. Whichever cover loses, you can use to create an alternative cover version so it doesn't go to waste, but choose the clickiest cover for your book's main page.

Use your fans. If you have a decent-sized fanbase, you might like to add a poll or simply ask for opinions about different cover options. Make sure to ask the designer for permission first – some don't like to have draft projects available for public viewing.

As I've mentioned in previous chapters, be wary when asking readers for their opinions. Remember, readers lie. They might choose the cover that stands out the most to them, but if they saw that same cover on an Amazon page and they didn't know you were the author, would they pick it up?

The only true way readers tell you what they want is through their purchases. I think testing an FB ad with two covers is going to be more effective than asking your readers, but this is still an option for you.

Do a cover reveal. A great piece of social media content is to reveal your cover to your readers in a post. This helps get them excited about the book before it's even live.

YOUR BOOK BLURB

Once the reader clicks on your book cover, they're taken to a product page where your blurb has to entice them to read the book. Writing blurbs isn't easy (I find them harder than writing the actual book!) but it's an essential skill to master if you want to sell books.

Your blurb is a short (150-250 words) description of your book to entice readers to hit BUY, or at least open the cover and take a look inside. Your blurb isn't a summary of the book – no, no, no, no. Instead, it gives the reader a sense of the main character, their key problem, the big bad looming danger on the horizon, and the genre of the book (aka, whether they can expect dragons or not. No surprise dragons. If there are dragons in your book, they should be on the cover, cuz dragons sell books. If there are no dragons, don't mention the dragons. You have been warned).

For non-fiction, your blurb will allow the reader to iden-tify with the problem they're having and see a way forward toward solving it, hopefully without medieval siege engines. You need to give them confidence you can solve it (usually by explaining your credentials) and show them what they can expect on the other side.

I like to begin my blurb with a short, snappy one-sentence

hook. Amazon will show this on its product search pages, so it's a great way to hook readers. I'll often use short phrases to list things that readers will encounter in the book. Lists of three or five problems are common in blurbs.

Blurbs are traditionally strictly in the third person, but I write mine mostly in the first person. I like throwing the reader right into that character's voice. Also, my books are mostly written in the first person, so I like that the voices of the blurb and book match.

In saying this, when I tested four blurbs for Fangs for Nothing, my most popular book to date, the third-person blurb won by an overwhelming majority. So I went with the data and used that blurb, and I haven't regretted it.

Your blurb is all about character – don't pack it full of plot elements. Instead, focus on helping readers get to know your protagonist and what messy jam they're going to get involved in.

Keep your blurb action-packed and full of conflict. You'll probably be focusing mainly on external conflict and consequences. The reader needs to sense the danger and understand why the danger is, well… dangerous. For certain genres in particular (romance, I'm looking at you), you might want to include a bit of that juicy internal conflict, as well.

Don't be afraid to mess with the format of blurbs. Use single-word paragraphs for impact. Write the blurb in textspeak, if that relates to the book. Write a laundry list – my friend KT Strange did this in her bestselling book *Phoenixcry*. That is blurb perfection.

Book 1 of my Nevermore Bookshop series, *A Dead and Stormy Night*, used to have a very different blurb (it was in third person and focused on the mystery elements). I had a TikTok go viral in 2022 that pushed the book into the top 1000 in the Amazon store. I realised, "Hey, if this Tiktok encouraged so many people to pick up a book from an author they've never heard of before, then it must resonate with readers." So I made the Tiktok content into my blurb. Unsurprisingly, ever since that change, Nevermore Bookshop has been one of my bestsellers.

Include the common tropes of your genre to alert readers that they'll love your story. Tropes are reader shorthand for 'story crack' – aka, addictive books they can't put down. You can do this overtly, by actually listing tropes in your blurb. Romance books often do this, stating the book is a 'friends-to-lovers romance' or a 'secret-baby romance.' Even using 'micro-tropes' (a term coined on Booktok for smaller scenes or character traits in a book that readers love) can help readers learn that they'll love your book.

You should know the common tropes in your genre from reading widely within it. Look at sites like TV Tropes for ideas. Studying short-form reader videos on TikTok and Reels can help you identify tropes and microtropes you use.

Another way authors signal to readers that they'll love a book is to compare it to other known titles/pop culture references. Do this sparingly and carefully – make sure the comparison is a fair one, or readers won't trust you in the future. For example, in my Nevermore Bookshop Mysteries series, I've sometimes used the tagline 'Agatha Christie meets Black Books' as it combines the murder mystery elements with snarky book-centric humour.

For non-fiction, create rapport with your reader by welcoming them into your vision and showing them their future. What will their life be like once they've finished your book? Use snippets from reviews to show how your book has already changed lives. Fiction authors can also highlight reviews in their blurb – use short sentences to show that other readers are loving your book.

Workshop your blurb with other writers and test it on family and friends. Look at the structure of blurbs for other successful authors in your genre. Don't be afraid to tweak it to make it as exciting and high-stakes as possible.

Thriller/horror writer Adam Croft has a great book on writing 'killer' blurbs (I see what you did there, Adam). I also recommend you check Miss Snark – a NYC literary agent who sadly no longer blogs but has left her site live with an archive of thousands of posts where she critiques query letters (basically blurbs) with her own signature style. You will laugh so much, and by the end, you will have had a more thorough lesson in writing great blurbs than I could ever give you.

OPTIMIZE YOUR BLURB FOR AMAZON

Use keywords, tropes, and genre search terms in your blurb – this can help you be found in more searches, as well as alerting readers that they'll like your book. Don't go crazy, though – your blurb still needs to be enjoyable to read.

Use HTML code for bold, italics, heading levels, and line space to make your blurb easily scannable. Non-fiction titles, in particular, will often use bullet points for impact.

Some authors like to list out the other books in their series so readers can see the reading order. You may find this useful to help convert readers across books in a series. Again, don't get too complicated. Your blurb is not the place to explain how a multi-series world fits together.

NO MATTER YOUR PROJECT, TITLE + COVER + BLURB WILL GET YOU NOTICED

If your readers aren't digital, then these things still matter. It's important to understand how YOUR readers choose books. For example, if you're writing poetry, you're going to be focused on getting reviews, on visual social media like Instagram, and also looking for holidays around where your poetry is given as gifts. All these things still require a quality cover and an enticing title and blurb.

Some things may work in one format better than others. Some covers will sell incredibly well on the special edition fancypants book market that won't attract people in thumbnail form to an ebook.

HOW TO ROCK YOUR TITLE, COVER, AND BLURB:

- What's your book's title? Tell it to a couple of friends you trust and ask them what they think the book is about based on the title. If they can't guess the genre, it might be time to rethink.
- If you're going to write in a series, think about how to link your titles together with a pattern. You'll also need to come up with a series title. Again, run this past your friends or readers and see if they can guess the genre.
- Search your title and series title online and make sure you're not competing with a recently published popular book in your genre.
- Figure out your budget for book covers. Once you have this number in your head, hunt out a range of design options that fit your budget. (You need to know the budget first because this will impact what type of designer you each for – pre-made or custom). Start compiling a Pinterest board or folder of inspiration to show your designer.
- Write your blurb. Now write it again.
- WRITE YOUR BLURB AGAIN. Tear up the paper in frustration. Scream about how this writing thing isn't all it's cracked up to be. Have brilliant blurb idea in the shower.
- Workshop your blurb with other writers. You'll often find a second set of eyes will pick up things you miss. There are great blurb-critique groups on Facebook you can join.

- Look at your whole package together. Title + cover + blurb. Do they feel as polished, professional and *suitable for your genre* as you can make them? Do they sit beside current bestsellers in your categories and look damn fine? If so, you're almost ready for prime time.

CHAPTER 7
UPLOAD AND PUBLISH – THE NUTS AND BOLTS

THIS CHAPTER IS all about getting your book from a file on your desktop of a bunch of handwritten pages to a live product people can download and read.

CHOOSE YOUR FORMATS

One of the cool things about self-publishing is that it's brought back types of stories that haven't been popular before and opened doors for alternative formats to flourish. It's worthwhile considering if you might be interested in publishing across multiple formats.

First of all, you've got ebooks. I recommend even if you're after print sales, you should have an ebook because it's free to publish and you might be surprised how many people buy them. The interesting thing about the ebook is how it's enabled writers of different lengths to enjoy success.

Traditional publishers have certain word count expectations they stick to – they want novels for adults to be between 60,000-90,000 words, fantasy tomes can be up to 120,000, category romance 40-55,000, YA around 40,000-70,000, etc. If a book falls too far out of these expected lengths, the publisher will likely pass. Too long, and the book will cost too much for the publisher to print. They'll either have to price it higher (meaning fewer people will buy it) or eat into their margins. Too short, and the book won't look like good value to readers viewing it on a store bookshelf. They'll choose something that costs the same but gives them more story for their bucks.

But with a digital market, the length of a book isn't an immediate, tactile sensation. The price of your book is set by you, and it doesn't have to correlate to length. Because of this, authors like H. M. Ward, Hugh Howey, etc have done well with shorter serials. Other authors are publishing epic 300,000-word science fiction tomes and raking in high page reads in KU. Some of the top indie authors on Amazon publish short travel guides or prepper manuals. Think about how you might be able to play with length for your audience.

You can use internal links in ebooks to lead readers around the book. Authors are experimenting with pick-a-path books where the readers can make certain choices that lead to other chapters, a great idea being carried to the next level by developers of interactive fiction apps.

Audiobooks are a growth area where indies are seeing a lot of success. The initial cost can be huge - expect $2,000 and up in production costs for a full-length book. If your books are already doing well, audio can be a good secondary income stream.

I've signed deals with audiobook publishers for several books, and I've also paid for audio to be produced myself. I'm enthusiastic about audio because I see it as such a huge potential for authors and because it's an accessible format that allows blind and low-vision readers a chance to access a wide library of stories.

In print, you have all the options a publisher has available. Print-on-demand often lacks the polish of a publisher, but for many types of books that doesn't matter. We've already spoken about opportunities for self-publishing in print in the previous chapter.

And then, of course, you have writers completely outside the traditional book structure. Think about story apps, comic books, movies, mixing writing with VR, anything you can imagine. My friend Felicity Banks/Louise Curtis writes interactive fiction and escape rooms. She landed the gig in part because of her track record as a fiction author.

KU OR WIDE?

This is an ebook only consideration, but as the majority of your sales will likely be digital, this is probably the most important decision you make about your book's future.

Will you put your book in Kindle Unlimited (KU)?

KU is Amazon's 'Spotify for books.' Readers love it because they can binge-read as many books as they want for a set fee. For the 'whale readers' who abound in genre fiction, KU is a blessing from the Reading Gods.

For authors, KU offers three advantages:

- Access to a large pool of hungry readers, many of whom will only read KU books.
- Readers feel as though KU books are 'free,' so they're more likely to take a chance on a new author.
- Access to KU-only marketing features, including free days (the ability to set your book to free for five days every three months) and Kindle Countdown Deals (where you can discount your book for up to 7 days and still keep 70% of the royalties, even if the book is $0.99).
- Preferential treatment in Amazon's algorithm. We know that Amazon encourages buyers to read

books in KU so that they have more exclusive
content than other retailers. We don't know exactly
what that looks like, but it is a thing.

If you want your ebook in KU, **it must be exclusive to
Amazon**. You can sell the paperback and audiobook in other
places, but not the ebook. Also, you don't get paid a royalty
as you do for a sale. Amazon pays a tiny fraction of a cent for
every 'page' a reader reads.

Amazon has an algorithm that builds a standardized page
count across all books – this is called KENPC (Kindle Edition
Normalized Page Count) and stops authors from using giant
fonts and other formatting tricks to inflate their page count.

KU has a 'pot' of money each month (made from the
money paid by KU subscribers) and Amazon divides that pot
by the total pages read to arrive at their per-page-read rate.
They will usually top up the pot with an influx of cash each
month to keep the rate between $0.004-$0.0049 (Yup, that's
less than half a cent per page).

Sounds complicated? It is. What can I say? You get used to
it. When random people overhear me talking to fellow
authors they must think we're speaking a different language.

KU has become such a force in the marketplace that KU
readers have their own trends, preferred genres, and reading
habits. Tropes, genres, and cover styles that do well wide
might sink in KU, and vice versa. Generally speaking, KU
readers read more books per month, they read genre fiction,
and they are more responsive to hot trends.

Many authors have built successful careers and multi-
million dollar businesses writing for KU readers. The biggest
downside is that you're only building readership in one
market. You're relying solely on Amazon – if they make
changes to the program or drop it (or you) completely, then
your income will suffer.

(It's useful to remember that just because you're a KU author, doesn't mean you don't diversify your income streams. My ebooks are exclusive to KU and my income comes from KU reads, ebook sales, paperback sales from Amazon, B&N, and Ingram Spark, paperback and special edition hardcover sales from my website, Kickstarter campaigns, merch drops, audiobooks, translations, paperback and hardcover sales at author signings, speaking, licensing, and traditional publishing deals.)

Going wide (having your books available on Apple Books, B&N, Kobo, Google Play, etc, as well as Amazon) gives you more of a safety net because you spread your risk. There's also less competition on the other platforms (and you'll still be earning royalties from sales on Amazon), and if you can nail your covers and genre, you'll find your books will be 'stickier' (retain regular sales volume) for longer.

On the downside, you miss out on tapping into the voracious KU readership. In certain genres, this can make it difficult to stand out. You'll have to spread your efforts across five platforms instead of laser-focusing on Amazon only. You may find it more difficult to find readers willing to take a chance on a new author.

While success is possible on both platforms, wide usually takes longer to build. Many wide authors choose this path because they've seen Amazon make changes with no notice that tank an author's career overnight, or they've had too many issues with Amazon's bots taking down books. They need the 'security' of an audience on the other platforms to keep their mental health intact and stress levels low.

You can do a little of both. Some people put new books into KU and then pull them wide after the page reads start to die down. Other authors launch wide for two weeks, then pull their books from the other platforms to place in KU. Some authors are KU in one pen name, wide with another.

My non-fiction (like this book) is all wide, and I have been wide with Steffanie Holmes in the past.

Whether you want to try KU is up to you – there is no right or wrong answer. Consider the following points:

- Are your readers in KU? If you write in a KU-heavy genre, it's best to at least start by going where the readers are.
- Can you deal with placing all your trust/hopes on Amazon?
- Can you deal with the additional hassle of publishing your books on multiple platforms?

Remember, your KU term only lasts 90 days, so it's worth at least experimenting with KU to see what it's like.

GOING WIDE: DIRECT VS AGGREGATORS

If you choose to go wide, you can do it in one of two ways – by uploading your books to each platform yourself, or by using an aggregator.

An aggregator allows you to upload your book once. In exchange for a percentage of your royalties, the aggregator will then place your book on all the different sales platforms. If you have to make changes to that book (for example, uploading a new file to fix some typos or placing the book on sale) you can do it from the aggregator's platform and they'll publish the changes across all vendors.

Draft2Digital is the aggregator I use – I use them for B&N (because you couldn't go direct as a New Zealand author when I started self-publishing), library databases like Hoopla and OverDrive, and some smaller marketplaces like Tolino and Scribd. They make things super easy, and I recommend them!

For Apple, Kobo, and Google Play, I'm direct. This allows

me to keep the majority of my royalties and also allows me access to merchandising opportunities from the individual vendors (by this I mean the vendor will promote my book. Kobo, in particular, has an awesome dashboard of monthly promotional opportunities you can apply for. You cannot access these through Draft2Digital).

I recommend being direct with Amazon for sure – it's likely to be your biggest earner. For the other platforms, do what you think is right for you. If I recommended one to be direct, it would be Kobo because of the promotions dashboard. Apple is my second-highest earning platform, so it's good to know I'm not giving away 10% of my royalties there.

UPLOADING TO YOUR WEBSITE

As a wide author, you may decide you'd like to sell ebooks directly to your readers. You can do this by setting up a website with a shopping cart (Shopify is most common) and allowing readers to buy your books from you. Authors call this 'direct sales.'

Direct sales are growing in the indie author world, and offer an exciting opportunity for authors who prefer ecome-Commerceategies over indie publishing strategies. The advantages of selling direct are numerous:

- You aren't giving a percentage of your earnings to a platform like Amazon or Apple.
- You keep all customer information across the whole transaction.
- You're able to use e-commerce tools and strategies to grow and retain your customer base without relying on the retailers.

But there are disadvantages:

- Running a direct sales store involves a steep learning curve, because you need to learn/understand ecommerce principles and set up your store, and you've got to get a ton of things right or you'll be turning readers away without even knowing it.
- With direct sales, you will burn through your current readers very quickly, and you'll need to find new ones. The retailers have strategies that are constantly bringing new readers to your page/search, but with a direct store, you'll need to do this yourself. This means that to keep new readers buying from your online store, you will need to spend money/time on advertising.
- With direct sales, you're in charge of shipping books (digital and physical), compliance, sales tax, and customer service. All those these things can be complicated and time-consuming.

Direct sales of ebooks tend to work better when you have several books you can offer in a bundle, or an ebook as a lead magnet to a higher-cost offering, such as a course. If you're interested in selling direct, I recommend checking out Morgana Best's FB group, Authors Going Direct. Morgana runs a direct sales course which we've found excellent!

(If you're in KU, you can still offer your books in a direct store, but since you can't sell ebooks, you'll be focusing on physical book sales or maybe audio).

UPLOADING TO A VENDOR

For ebooks, there are five main vendors; Amazon, Apple Books, Barnes & Noble, Kobo, and Google Play. There are also several smaller stores such as Smashwords, Tolino, and

Scribd, as well as stores like OverDrive specifically for libraries.

Remember, if you opt to enrol your books in Kindle Unlimited, you must remain exclusive to Amazon. If you're wide, you should have your books on as many platforms as possible. Wide authors often make up their income with small amounts of sales from lots of different platforms.

You'll need to sign up for an account at each vendor and give them the required tax information and bank details so they can pay your royalties. Whether you're uploading to Amazon, Kobo or any other vendor, you're going to see roughly the same fields to fill in to upload a book. Here's what each field means.

TITLE

The title of your book. This has to match the title on your cover. Choose an exciting title that represents your genre and offers readers an enticing hint at what they might discover inside.

SUBTITLE

If you have a subtitle you can add this here. Sometimes people like to include some indication of the book's genre. For example, I sometimes use 'a paranormal reverse harem' on my romance books. On some vendors, you're only allowed to do this if the subtitle appears on your book cover.

SERIES NAME

The name of the series. For example, 'Nevermore Bookshop Mysteries.'

SERIES NUMBER

The sequence of the book in the series.

EDITION

Sometimes, you might update a book. Leave blank unless you're uploading a significant update to a book.

AUTHOR

That's you! Make sure you use the name you want to be public.

CONTRIBUTORS

Other authors, contributors, or illustrators (if you're writing a children's book). You don't have to add your cover artist or editor unless their name will mean something to your audience. If you're uploading a translation, it's common practice to name the translator in this section.

DESCRIPTION

This is your blurb. We've spoken about blurbs at length in the last chapter, so you should be good to go. Use the available formatting tools/coding to add bold, subheadings, and italics.

ISBN

This is an International Standard Book Number – an identification number used by the publishing industry to help distinguish and locate books. Each ISBN identifies the country, region, or language of the book, the publisher, the format and title.

You do not require an ISBN to self-publish, but if part of your publishing plan involves being stocked in bookstores or libraries, it might be worth considering. In your country, there will be an issuing body that takes care of allocating ISBNs. In some countries – like New Zealand, yay! – ISBNs are free, while other places will incur a small fee. You need one ISBN for each format, so a book released in ebook, print, and audio will need three ISBNs in total. If you do a second edition of your book with changes or a different cover, you'll require a new ISBN.

PUBLISHER OR IMPRINT

Some vendors will allow you to add your own publishing house to this field. If you don't fill in this field, it will auto-populate with the vendor's self-publishing arm. Many indies like to invent their own publisher or imprint because it looks more professional. I have an 'imprint' for my fiction (Bacchanalia House) and one for my non-fiction (Rage Against the Manuscript).

LANGUAGE

Choose the language you've used for the majority of the book.

PUBLISHING RIGHTS

You'll be asked if you own the copyright for your work or if it's a public domain work (for example, if you're publishing *Pride & Prejudice*, this is public domain).

AGE/GRADE RANGE

Use this only if your book is for a junior market. Otherwise, leave it in adult even if it's YA, as many adults read YA.

ENABLE DRM

I've spoken about DRM in an earlier chapter. I always choose 'no.'

CATEGORIES

Categories are a key tool for readers to discover new authors they love. Many readers use categories to browse their favourite genre online and see which books take their fancy. For this reason, it's important to place your book in the correct categories.

On Amazon, you can currently choose three categories. Some other sites allow a different number of categories. You want to choose the categories where your readers will be most likely to search for your books.

For example, if you've written a supernatural urban fantasy, you want to put it in fiction > fantasy > urban, and maybe fiction > mystery/suspense > supernatural, and not in non-fiction > occult and supernatural. The people searching that category are looking for books on true hauntings and Wiccan rituals, not fantasy novels.

Most books will fit neatly within at least one category. For example, my books are most definitely fiction > romance > paranormal. For your second category, try to choose something different to help you get in front of a wider number of readers – so perhaps instead of choosing a second romance category for my Nevermore books, I list it in a mystery category.

Choose the most specific category possible. Your book will

appear in all the main branches of your category. For example, if I choose fiction > romance > paranormal > vampires, my book can be found by people browsing the general romance category AND the general paranormal category. However, if I just choose fiction > romance, readers won't find my book in the paranormal or vampire category unless I use keywords to get there.

KEYWORDS

After categories come keywords. These are words readers type into the search box to find books they might enjoy. You want to include as many potential words and phrases as possible to help readers (and the vendor's algorithms) understand what's inside your book.

On Amazon, you have seven slots for keywords. However, you can use more than one keyword in each slot. You have 50 characters in the slot and you can use every one. Choose words readers looking for a story like yours might want to choose. Focus on the main elements and tropes in your story. You can also use keywords to get into categories you weren't able to use in your category selection, so choose as many of these as fit your book. Amazon provides a list of categories with keyword requirements.

Authors use various techniques to research and test their keywords. Good keywords may include words that describe your genre, common tropes and micro-tropes in your book, words that describe a character or an experience the reader wants to have, and sometimes even common misspellings. Kindlepreneur has a great article on how to use your keywords and choose the best ones. I recommend giving it a read.

PRE-ORDER/RELEASE NOW

You can choose to release your book as soon as the vendor approves it or put it up for pre-order. If you choose to make a book available for pre-order, this means readers can opt to reserve a copy of the book now for a release date in the future. They will be charged on release day, and all the sales royalties for the pre-order book will hit your account on that same day.

According to research conducted by David Gaughran, on Amazon, you're given a boost in ranking on release day – this boost depends on how many pre-orders you have and how long ago the reader ordered the book. On other vendors, the boost can be even higher. Having a popular book with a ton of pre-orders can help you rock a great launch. However, if you don't think you'll get a decent amount of pre-orders, it's usually better to wait until release day to go live on Amazon.

All the vendors that allow you to create pre-orders do them up to a year in advance without the need for a completed book. This can give you time to organize launch activities and advertising and is great for encouraging read-through on your series. The best time to convince readers to buy the next book in your series is immediately after they've finished the last book. This is how I use pre-orders. Occasionally, if I'm writing a super trendy book or if I have a certain type of promotion I'll put the pre-order for book 1 up to capture readers desperate for more in that trend.

Just remember that putting up a pre-order is making a promise to your readers that you'll have a book ready on that date. If you constantly move or delete pre-orders, it sends a message to your readers that they can't trust you. Amazon will also give you a penalty for moving or cancelling a pre-order. So make sure you're ready to launch before you put up that pre-order!

TERRITORIES

You can decide if your book will be available worldwide or only in certain countries. This is mainly for people who may have sold the publishing rights to a certain territory but are self-publishing in others. I'd choose 'worldwide' unless you have a contractual reason not to.

On most vendors, you're able to set country-specific pricing. Some (Amazon, Kobo) will automatically populate prices based on current exchange rates. I always go through these prices and tidy up the numbers. (For example, if Canada converts to $4.72 I'll change it to $4.99, etc).

PRICE

Set the price for your book.

As we've already discussed, one of the key advantages of self-publishing ebooks is the ability to offer cheaper books to voracious readers. Amazon knows that readers buy more books during a specific price range – that's why they encourage self-publishers to price between $2.99-9.99 by offering 70% royalties. Outside of this range, a book on Amazon will only receive 35% royalties.

Ideally, you want to price as high as you can before readers stop buying your book. Many self-publishers will have their first book at $0.99 to entice people to try it. You have to sell six times as many books at $0.99 as you do at $2.99 to make the same amount of money, so I don't like this strategy myself, but you can always try it.

Wide authors have another pricing option called Permafree. This is where you set the first book in your series permanently free, and use that as a loss leader to draw readers into your series. Permafree only works if a book is an intro into a series, and the more cliffhangery your ending is, the better it works.

You can set your book to free on Apple, Kobo, Google Play, and B&N, either by going direct or by using an aggregator like Draft2Digital. Amazon doesn't have an option to set your book free (unless you're in Kindle Unlimited, and you can set your book free for 5 days out of 90, but then you'd be exclusive to Amazon). You can get a book set free on Amazon by publishing it free on the other vendors. Amazon hates for other vendors to beat them on price, so they will 'price match' your book to free.

It will usually take a couple of days for Amazon to notice and match the lower price. You can hurry them along by going to the 'report a lower price' on the book's product page and linking your free book from another retailer.

UPLOAD YOUR FILE

Here you upload your book file in epub format. You can also upload a normal docx file formatted with styles – the uploader will convert it into epub.

The program will kick back if there are any errors in your files, and you'll want to use the preview option to make sure everything has come out the way you want it. (This is especially important for print).

UPLOAD YOUR COVER FILE

Do the thing! Make sure your cover file meets the minimum dimension requirements. For Amazon, this is 2,560 x 1,600 pixels. The minimum image **size** allowed is 1,000 x 625 pixels – that's probably gonna look a bit shite, though. The maximum image **size** allowed is 10,000 x 10,000 pixels, but you don't need to make it that big. Your **cover** image has gotta be less than 50MB.

CHECK YOUR FILES

Vendors allow you to download their files to your reading device or check on your screen. I highly recommend you take a look, especially for your print book.

PUBLISH

Hit that button. You're ready!

Most vendors advise they take around 72 hours to approve your book for publishing, but most of mine go live in a few hours.

PRINT BOOKS

Now that you've been through the process with an ebook, you can transfer much of the same info over to your print version.

For print, you have two options – you can either use print-on-demand or a printing company.

Print-on-demand means when someone orders your book from Amazon, Amazon (or another vendor) will then print one copy of that book and send it off to that person. You don't have to be involved in the process. You carry no inventory and you don't have to pay anything upfront – you'll see a royalty every time a reader purchases a book.

The disadvantage is that the books tend to have a more expensive list price because there are no economies of scale. You're able to order author copies of your book at cost, but if you're ordering them to sell in person, the higher production cost will eat into your potential profit margin. If you live in a country like New Zealand, far away from the print-on-demand centre, you'll end up losing even more of your potential profit from shipping costs. Print-on-demand books also tend to be lower quality, and you won't have as many formatting and fancy embellishment options (although this is changing).

If you plan to hand-sell a lot of print copies at conventions, events, or shows, it might be worthwhile to do a **print run** with a local printer. Printing 100-500 copies and storing them in your garage until you need them will mean that the per-unit cost is lower. Shipping will probably cost less, too (especially if you choose a local company), so you'll have more profit per book.

For higher volumes, you can also choose to do an offset print run. These are usually done through printers in China or Eastern Europe, although there are lots of printers all over the world. An offset print run allows for economy of scale. I use offset printers for my special edition books. I can print 1000+ hardcover books for a per-book cost of $5-7 with all the fancypants embellishments. But I need to be patient, as these books take months to print and arrive at my fulfilment centre. And I need to have a high-volume order to make the printing worthwhile. Offset is probably not an option you'll be looking at for your first books. It all depends on your strategy.

I recommend you do both a short print run and print-on-demand if you need print copies to hand-sell. You can use the same ISBN for both versions. If you don't do events and the majority of your customers will be online (like mine), you won't need the local print run.

POD SERVICES

Several companies provide print-on-demand services. The two most commonly used by self-publishers are KDP Print and IngramSpark. A newer company servicing the POD market is Bookvault, who have a POD system you can integrate with your website, and they also offer several embellishments via their Bookvault Bespoke line, such as printed edges and foil, for short print runs.

KDP Print and Ingramspark will manage books on Amazon, and if you tick a box for 'expanded distribution,' they will manage your POD books on other retailers worldwide and make them available to libraries and bookstores. Ticking expanded distribution will add a couple of dollars to the overall cost of producing each book.

My strategy: I use KDP Print for Amazon only. It's super easy to use. You can create print books from the same KDP dashboard you use for ebooks, and it will pre-populate details from your ebook over to your print book (and vice versa) so you don't have to repeat everything.

Not ticking expanded distribution on Amazon allows me to get my books to a lower price point while still making a decent return from my royalties. Since Booktok became a thing, my print sales have increased and are now a decent chunk of my monthly earnings.

I then upload the same book with the same ISBN to IngramSpark and B&N (for distribution to Barnes and Noble stores only). I use IngramSpark for expanded distribution, but not to Amazon (because KDP Print takes care of that). I also buy author copies from IngramSpark as they are closer to me in New Zealand so it's cheaper.

This is a complex way of doing things that works for me because I'm trying to maximize profit on Amazon – my biggest platform – while also making my print books available as widely as possible (diversification hooray!). It's a win/win for my specific situation. Your situation and your success metrics may vary.

For uploading your print copy to a service, most of the fields will be the same between print/ebook – title, description, categories, etc. Here are a few specific to print:

LARGE PRINT

Readers with a print disability may like to have a paperback version with a font size they can read. In certain genres, this is in hot demand – such as cosy mysteries where the audience skews older. Amazon allows you to provide this by making 'large print' an option you can use – you can link it with your other formats through Author Central and it will sync your reviews. It acts as a separate book entry and will need its own ISBN.

A good font size to use is 16-point. If you're going to do large print, opt for a large trim size. 6x9 will help keep your pages down if you usually print in 5x8. It's a good idea to have your designer add a banner or star that reads 'large print edition' on the cover.

Vellum can now auto-generate a large-print version of your print book. Otherwise, you'll need to manually format it.

INTERIOR PAPER

You can choose from black/white or colour printing (colour will be more expensive), and white or cream paper. I opt for cream paper because to me white looks too stark. White is the best option for books with lots of images, as it shows off colour and contrast with increased vibrancy.

You'll have to let your cover designer know your paper choice because white/cream papers have a different thickness (called GSM) that will slightly change the width of your book's spine.

You cannot change this once you've published.

TRIM SIZE

This is the size of your book. Novels have standard trim sizes for trade paperbacks – most are 5x8, 5.25x8, 5.5x8.5, or 6x9. If your novel is shorter, try a smaller size so it has more pages. If your novel is longer, try a larger size so it's less bulky.

Manuals and workbooks are usually larger – 8x10, 8.5x11. General non-fiction is usually 6x9. Kids' picture books are 8x10 or 10x8 but can be a whole range of sizes. Artbooks can be whatever size you want. Any book can be whatever size you want – I'm just trying to help you narrow it down.

You cannot change this once you've published.

BLEED

'Bleed' is how close images get to the edge of the page. If you have images that reach right to the edge of the pages, add bleed to your book so that your images don't end up with a white border around them when the book is trimmed. For a 6x9 book, you'd usually set bleed to around 6.125x9.25. Talk to your designer if you're feeling confuzzled.

You cannot change this once you've published.

COVER TYPE

You'll usually have two options – matte or glossy. Glossy is a shiny surface. If your cover has a lot of black, this will make it look darker. It will often make artwork appear more striking. Children's books, non-fiction and anything art will usually go gloss. Matte doesn't have the sheen and looks quite sophisticated. It's typical for novels/fiction/poetry books.

You cannot change this once you've published.

EXPANDED DISTRIBUTION

Tick if you want your book to be distributed to library and bookstore catalogues, as well as to other online retailers (but just because it's distributed does not mean it will be purchased).

AUDIO

Audiobooks are one of the fastest-growing segments of the publishing market. A massive influx of readers discovered audiobooks during the COVID-19 pandemic, and they're now addicted to listening to books whenever they can. People are now streaming audio to their devices and listening to audiobooks on Echo, Alexa and Google Home. There are audio subscription packages similar to KU, and with Amazon's Whispersync, you can read your book at a coffee shop, and then when you hop into your car the audio will start playing from the page you finished reading. It's so rad.

It's worth considering getting your books in audio if you think there's a market for your words.

Right now, there's an opportunity to stand out in audio because there isn't as much selection as there is for print and ebooks. There are a few different options for publishing audio – the main three used by indies are ACX, Findaway Voices, and Author's Republic. These act both as production houses (helping to pair you up with a narrator and manage the recording of your book) and as distribution (getting your book onto the platforms and managing royalties).

On ACX, you're able to choose a narrator with the following two options – you can pay the full amount of the production (an amount per finished hour) upfront and keep the entire royalty. Or you can pay nothing upfront and split the royalties with your narrator.

On Author's Republic, you can put up a project and audition narrators from their roster, or upload and distribute a finished audiobook. Narrators set their own per-finished-hour rate and this needs to be paid in full after approving the audio. Author's Republic also offers a turnkey service where one of their producers will take care of the entire process for you. The cost for this is a USD$250 Fee + $349 per finished hour of audio.

Findaway Voices used to provide narrator auditions but now only allows for uploading finished books and distributing them.

You can also create the audiobook yourself (either by hiring your own narrator or narrating yourself) and upload it to your chosen platform.

If using ACX, you'll also need to decide if you want to be exclusive. This gives you higher royalties but means your books won't be available anywhere else apart from Amazon, Audible, and iTunes. Author's Republic and Findaway Voices distributes to several other retailers (Findaway Voices is owned by Spotify). It's up to you which you think is best. Findaway Voices also offers Chirp deals, which is a promotion where you apply to offer your audiobook cheap for a limited time to encourage new readers to try your books.

For more tips about audio, check out this episode of the Creative Penn podcast about audio rights and production with author J. Daniel Sawyer, or Karen Commins' audiobook marketing cheat sheet.

HOW TO ROCK MAKING YOUR BOOK LIVE:

- Decide which formats you'll use for launch. Ebook and print should be a must. Anything else?
- KU or wide – what's your poison?
- If you're going wide, choose which platforms you'll be using directly. If you're like me and you live in

New Zealand, you may find that sometimes the choice is made for you.

- Lockdown book information like your title, subtitle, description, series name, etc.
- Sort yourself some ISBNs if you're gonna use 'em.
- Choose your two categories. Choose them well.
- Find keywords relevant to your readership.
- Decide if you're doing a pre-order. You'll need to have a cover and blurb prepared to upload immediately.
- Upload – get to know the process for each format on the different quirks of each system.
- Pick your pricing strategy for book 1/your whole series. Reserve the right to change your mind later.
- Check everything is A-OK before you hit publish! Check it again! You want this launch to be perfection!

CHAPTER 8
LAUNCH WITH A BANG!

YOUR BOOK LAUNCH is one of the best marketing tools you have. Reader interest is usually highest during the launch, and retailers give your book extra attention, so you should take advantage of this and do a big marketing push.

For the next few guidelines, you need to take off your author and publisher hats and put on your fancy-schmancy marketing hat. It can be hard to think like a marketer when you have no marketing background. You don't want to be scammy. You don't want to 'bother' people.

Remember that you're only bothering people if you're contacting them out-of-the-blue asking them to buy a book they have no interest in. Marketing isn't like that these days – no one wants to waste time or money or energy on people who don't want our shit. What we do now is wait for people to indicate "This is something I'm interested in" and then we can say, "Oh, that's so cool! Me too. You might like my book." And you can remind them about it because when you want something but you forgot to buy it right away, reminders are useful!

There are people in the world who are genuinely waiting for exactly the book you've created. Think about how excited you are when you hear your favourite author has released a new book. You're grateful you heard about the release so you can grab it RIGHT NOW. That's how people feel about your book. Isn't that awesome?

Telling people who are interested in your work that you've got something new out isn't scammy. Trying to convince people who AREN'T interested that they need your book, over and over again – that *is* scammy. Telling them you've written a book and then selling them a toaster – that might be scammy, or just plain odd. You? Not scammy.

So don't worry so much. And remember that as much as this marketing stuff can seem a little strange and difficult and scary, it's how you get to connect with readers – which is basically the most fun thing about being an author apart from the actual writing bit.

First, you need to decide what day to launch. You don't need to put too much thought into this beyond making sure the book is actually finished :) Do try to steer clear of public and school holidays, and elections. During these times people are busy with family and other commitments and aren't paying attention to new books.

Design your launch around your readers. Focus on activities that will alert any current audience you have about your book, and that will bring in new readers interested in your title.

Here are some things to consider:

- What formats do you want to launch with? Ebook, print, audio, other formats like workbooks, large print, or special edition.
- Will you do a pre-order? Only some platforms allow pre-orders. I like to have a pre-order so I have somewhere to direct people when I'm marketing pre-launch. If you don't do a pre-order, I'd at least

have a mailing list with maybe the first few chapters as a free download.

- Do you need to hire someone or coordinate other people/details? For example, are you using a publicist? Are you doing a collaborative launch with another author? Are you sending out physical ARC copies or PR boxes? Do you need to wait for your cover designer to finish book 2's cover so you can put that up for pre-order first?

PREPARING FOR LAUNCH

Here are a few activities you absolutely should do before your book launches.

CLAIM YOUR BOOK IN AUTHOR CENTRAL

Author Central is a hub for your books on Amazon. It gives you an author page – when a reader clicks on your name, they'll see a list of your books, a bio, and a feed of news and social media posts. Making an Author Central page is a simple way to increase your visibility and sell-through on Amazon.

To create an Author Central page, you'll need to sign up your pen name to authorcentral.amazon.com. Then, upload your books. You need to create a page in each territory – US, UK, AU, FR, etc – and add your books, a bio, an author photo, and links to social media/blog feeds for news. These days, Amazon usually automatically adds your books to your Author Central pages, but not always, so it pays to check.

CREATE A MULTILINK

It gets tedious writing out every store link for your book every time you talk about it. Added to this problem, if you send readers to an Amazon page outside their territory (for example, if you give the US link to readers in Australia) it will look as though your book isn't available. Multilinks solve this issue, as well as allow you to gather additional information.

I use Books2Read.com to create my links. There are lots of other companies that provide links specifically for authors (ReaderLinks is another one I've seen around, and Genius Links is another people love). I like Books2Read because they're affiliated with Draft2Digital, who are awesome.

ADD YOUR LINKS TO YOUR AUTHOR'S WEBSITE AND SOCIAL MEDIA

Got your multilink? Good – now make a page for your book on your website and any social media profiles you have and direct readers where to grab it!

SEND OUT AN ARC TO REVIEWERS

Early reviews can be one factor in a book's success. Social proof is an important part of the psychology of shopping – we like to purchase things and read books that others already love because it makes us feel as though we're in a super-secret club. We trust the opinions of others – even people we don't know – to point us towards things we'll enjoy.

If a reader sees a book already has several 4-5 star reviews, they'll know other people have read and enjoyed that book, and it'll make them more likely to take a chance on it even if you're a new author to them.

If they land on your author page and see no reviews, they might assume your book isn't worth their time. That's why it's a good idea to focus some of your pre-launch efforts on building a team of reviewers who could be counted on to place reviews as soon as your books come out.

Some promotion companies (such as BookBub) need to see

reviews on a book before you can book their services. There's also evidence that the number and quality of reviews count toward ranking and algorithmic advantages on some of the stores (where and how much is a mystery).

This is why it's a good idea to send out Advance Reader Copies (ARCs) of your book to reviewers before your launch date, so they have a chance to read it and are ready to review on release day.

If you want to do ARCs, you'll need to find reviewers, and you'll want those reviewers to be VERY likely to enjoy your book (so readers of your genre who've given favourable reviews of similar books to yours before).

In the first instance, you could talk to friends or family members who read in your genre and ask if they'd be interested in being an advance reader. You want to make sure these are amazing supportive people because you need those first reviews to land on your book to be 4-5 stars.

(NB: Sometimes, Amazon will remove reviews if they conclude they've come from friends and family – ie. reviews from people who are your friends on Facebook. It's always best to try to cultivate reviewers from readers, but we all have to start from somewhere.)

If there are reader groups or forums for your genre, you may collect a few advance readers by posting there.

You might also like to chat with other author friends who write in the same genre and might be interested in a review swap. Personally, I feel a conflict of interest as an author writing product reviews on other books, so I don't do it. Other authors don't feel that way, so you may find someone excited to swap reviews with you. Alternatively, you could swap blurb quotes – these aren't the same as a review – they're a marketing quote that goes on your book's cover, front pages, or Amazon page.

A big site for sourcing ARC reviews is NetGalley. This is where most reviewers will have an account, and big publishers as well as indie authors post their books for review. I had over six hundred reviewers request Fangs for Nothing when I put it up on NetGalley. This site is very expensive to use as an individual, but there are indie author Netgalley Co-Ops you can use to get your book in Netgalley for a month or two for a much lower rate.

You can also message booktokers, bookstagramers or other bookish people on social media in your genre to see if they'd like an ARC copy. Write them a personal note that makes it clear you understand their content and don't harass them if they don't reply or ask for money for a review (some content creators consider these as paid advertising services they offer for authors and charge accordingly. It's up to you if you have a budget and think this is valuable).

There are also ARC services and sites like Hidden Gems and Booksprout that connect readers and reviews. These are often booked far in advance but can be a good option to get a strong influx of reviews.

I built my ARC team several years ago through my newsletter funnel. When readers signed up for my newsletter, they received a welcome email and a link to a free story or bonus scene. Then a few days later they'd receive a second email with some fun facts about me. A few days after THAT, they'd get an email asking if they'd like to join my ARC team. They'd get to read books for free a week before they're published, as long as they agree to write an honest review. After I acquired a hundred reviewers, I took away the email. Now, I only add new people to the team if they specifically contact me to ask (although I might add more in the future).

There are specific rules on Amazon about reviews. You cannot pay people to review your books. However, you are allowed to pay for a service to help you find reviewers, such as the ones I've already mentioned. Any site that guarantees a certain number of reviews with a certain star rating is running afoul of Amazon's TOS and could put your account in danger. Beware!

I used to manage my ARC requests manually, attaching and emailing a file with a personal message to everyone who replied. I'd send a reminder to review on the publication day, and another a week or two after that. Now I use a company called Booksprout to manage my ARCs. It auto-sends the reminder messages. It's awesome!

There are other ways to gain reviews without an ARC team, but they usually cost money or effort. There are blog tour companies and author PR firms that set up a tour for you around different book blogs or social accounts. Many offer book reviews from content creators as part of these tours, and some even offer review-only tours.

How many reviews is the right number? The answer to that question depends widely on what stage you're at in your author career, how many reviews similar books in your genre have, what readers expect from reviews, etc, etc. Some reviews are better than none, and better quality/higher star reviews are better than more reviews.

Ultimately, you should be looking to cultivate your own ARC team. Occasionally I have bloggers and reviewers asking me if they could join my team. I add them to the list.

ENDORSEMENTS/BLURBS

Endorsements are those little phrases on the front of a book from another author in your genre. They can be pretty tough to get if you're a brand-new author, and most self-published authors don't worry about them. However, if you happen to be friends with a big name in your genre and they're supportive of your work, ask them if they'd consider writing a blurb for you. You've got nothing to lose and everything to gain!

BUILDING AN AUDIENCE BEFORE YOU LAUNCH

Some authors will launch a new book on a brand new pen name and see it rocket straight to the top of the Amazon store. You can't count on this, of course. Remember my adage – I choose to believe I'm not going to be the exception.

If you're a brand new author and you want to make the biggest splash with the launch of your book, then you might want to start finding ways to build an audience *before* you launch. That way, you already know that as soon as you hit publish you'll have at least a few rabid fans ready to snap up your book. If your audience is big enough, it could give you a serious bump on Amazon that could result in the platform working to promote you to even *more* new readers.

Pre-building an audience sounds like a great idea!

In theory.

In reality, if you're not naturally marketing savvy and you're not already involved in audience-building activities (such as a non-fiction author on the speaker circuit or creating short-form videos about your genre) it can be rage-inducing.

If the thought makes you want to break out in hives, you don't have to do it. (Remember, if it's not fun, what's the point?) But if you think you could benefit from building an audience pre-launch, here are some ideas.

The key to any successful pre-launch is two-fold.

1. Give readers free content they can devour *right now*.
2. Give them a way to opt-in for *more* content in such a way that you capture information about them.

What kind of free content could you give away? Fiction authors will usually do either a sample of the book or a prequel short story. Non-fiction authors will use some book content to create a short guide. Poets can, of course, give away some poems, or perhaps an essay or video on the inspiration or themes behind the upcoming collection. Children's book authors will often do activity pages.

Free content could also include a podcast series relating to the topic of your book, Facebook posts in a private or public group, YouTube videos, or guest blog posts on popular websites. You are limited only by your imagination and your available time/resources. Also, try and keep your free content closely tied to your actual book.

Below, I give you some more ideas.

NON-FICTION

If you're releasing a non-fiction book on a certain topic, the best thing you can do is to create a ton of free content about that topic – a website full of articles, a podcast, and a YouTube channel. From that free content, give interested people a link to sign up for a mailing list to be notified when your book comes out.

FICTION

Fiction is a bit harder to create an audience before the book releases. One way writers do this is to put the book up for pre-order – this can work exceptionally well if your book is in a super-hot genre. You could also create a mailing list and give away a prequel story or sample of the book.

You can also adopt the same technique as for non-fiction and put up free content with links to join a mailing list. This works well for books with a theme you can speak about. For example, if you're writing a certain type of fantasy book, you could create a YouTube channel where you create content around that genre (book lists and top tens are popular on YouTube). I've listed heaps of ideas in the section below.

POETRY

Poetry has been experiencing a renaissance, fueled by social-media-savvy poets like Brian Bilston, Rupi Kaur, and my personal favourite, Nikita Gill. These 'instapoets' are largely traditionally published and account for 47% of poetry book sales in the US.

If you want to get noticed as a poet, it's a good idea to use social media as a platform. Combine your poetry with imagery to create shareable images. You can do a lot with poetry and music and video.

Allow and encourage your fans to repost and share your content. Include your social media handle on everything. Remember when you're on social media to adhere to the brand you've created for yourself – create a cohesive poetry experience so readers feel welcomed and comfortable returning to hear your beautiful words.

PROMOTING YOUR BOOK BEFORE AND DURING YOUR LAUNCH

The most important time for marketing your new book is during its launch month. Before your launch, you create excitement, collect pre-orders, and find potential readers. During launch, the most eyeballs will be on your book and the retailers will be promoting it to their audience.

Probably you started your launch plan well before your launch (hint: you should do this). When you plan your launch, you want to think about it as having two key parts:

a. Current audience. Make sure anyone who has followed any of your endeavours over the years knows you have a book out. The truth is that not all your readers are constantly following your social media, waiting with bated breath for the next release. You have to shout out loud multiple times to make sure they see you have a book.

b. New readers. Every launch you do should reach a few more new readers than the last, and you then funnel those readers into your new book and then into your fan audience.

Here are some strategies you can use to rock your book launch:

MAILING LIST

If you don't already have a mailing list, now is a good time to set one up. Most writers use services like Mailerlite or Mailchimp, however, there are literally hundreds to choose from. I use a company called Kit and I love them because it's all quite simple and there aren't lots of bells and whistles but it still does a lot.

Once your list is set up, link it in the back of your book, and readers will sign up to be alerted when you have a new release. I like to offer readers bonus content in exchange for their email addresses. This encourages more people to sign up.

I write a bonus piece of content for (nearly) every new series I publish. Usually, I will take a hooky or spicy scene from the book and rewrite it from another character's POV. This is super easy. Sometimes, like with the Grimdale Grave-yard series, something happened to the character's before the book's timeline that they discuss in the book, and I might write that scene. Other times, like with Fangs for Nothing, it might be a scene set after the events of the book (but not pivotal to the story). Lots of writers love an extra epilogue but I don't tend to do these as I write series with cliffhangers. I also will regularly create a playlist for a character in the book that I can also use as bonus content.

These bonus scenes are designed to appeal to readers who finished the story. They're not introductions for new readers.

I add each scene to a free ebook I have called *Cabinet of Curiosities*. This is what readers get when they sign up for the newsletter. So they don't just get their bonus scene, but all the other bonus scenes from all my other books. I have links to each book 1 in the bonus scenes and I can see that readers click on those links from the *Cabinet of Curiosities* book, so it does help a bit with sellthrough between series.

Most readers join my mailing list from the link in the back of my books (right underneath the TO BE CONTINUED, after I've linked to the pre-order for the next book), and from the pop-up on my website. I know people who sign up for my mailing list have either read a book of mine or know who I am and what I'm about enough to have gone to my website and signed up. I don't need to sell them on me – they already know and like my books.

Some authors like to build their newsletters from promo services or ads to free prequel books – these readers don't know who the author is, so once the reader has signed up, it's up to the author to introduce themselves and get the readers to buy their books. I prefer to keep my list only to readers who've actively joined because they love my books.

You can do both of these techniques – segment your news-letter so you introduce yourself to the new readers, and give different content to your readers who already know you.

If you already have readers on your mailing list, then you should alert them about your new release. About 6-8 weeks before release, I show them the cover and blurb. About a month before release, basically from the time I have a decent first draft, I start sending out weekly excerpts. I might also send funny lists or little "did you know" things about the books. I have a lot of fun trying to convince the readers they HAVE to read this book.

You can also ask other authors to promote your book to

their lists. We call this a 'newsletter swap'. It's most effective if the audience for your book and the other author's books is as close as possible. I have a few long-term author friends who I swap with regularly and it always adds a wee boost. This can take a bit of organizing but it can be a simple thing you can do to start promoting your book as a new author.

How often should you send emails? More often than you think. Lots of writers only send once a month. They worry about bothering people. I look at all the emails I get from stores I love, usually one every couple of days, and I don't feel like I'm bothering anyone. I want to have the best shot of readers seeing I have a new book out, so I tend to send newsletters roughly once a week, and 2-3 times a week during the week before and after a launch. How often you send is completely up to you.

If you do nothing else on this launch promotion list I've put together for you, you should do this one – create a mailing list and a free download to encourage readers onto it, and send emails to your mailing list.

SHORT-FORM VIDEO CONTENT (TIKTOK/REELS/YOUTUBE SHORTS, ETC)

I can't update a self-publishing book in 2024 without talking about TikTok.

The particular part of Tiktok known as "booktok" has become a force of nature in the publishing world, especially for genre fiction. Voracious readers have discovered the platform and are sharing their favourite books far and wide. As an author, you can get your videos in front of those readers and introduce new readers to your work.

TikTok is currently the **number one source of free traffic for romance authors.** There was a crazy time in 2022 when the top 100 on Amazon was nearly entirely made up of brand-new books that TikTok had made go viral. Several of my author friends owe their success to readers on Tiktok promoting their books for them. Algorithm changes and the Tiktok ban in the US mean this is tougher now, but short-form video content (whether on Tiktok or another app like Threads or Lemon8) is still an amazing way to promote your books to readers.

I'm not a video expert, and I haven't had the kind of wild success of TikTok many of my colleagues have. However, I have found new readers and improved my bottom line by approximately 30% thanks to sustained effort on TikTok and Reels over the last three years. Here are some things I have learned and tips I can share:

- TikTok/Reels are video apps. There are many different little "spaces" in the Tiktok/Reels ecosystem – no matter what kooky hobby you have or videos you like, there is a space for you. I love #poletok and #meadtok (spaces on Tiktok where people share their pole dance videos and their recipes for making mead). One of my friends loves TikTok videos of people icing cookies. It's a whole thing.
- Booktok is the space on Tiktok for book lovers. Bookstagram is the same space on Instagram. Bookthreads is that space on Threads. The majority of booktok is romance readers, although there are other genre readers there, too. Many of these readers are rediscovering their love of reading thanks to the app, and many of them read hardcovers and paperbacks instead of digital books. My print book sales have increased 700% (no, that's not a typo) since I started on Tiktok/Reels.
- You create a free creator account in TikTok. This is an account only for author stuff, so don't use it to

watch random stuff, as that confuses the algorithm. I have a separate account just for watching non-bookish stuff.

- Reels on Instagram are posted from your main account (to a different place than the main feed, although I also copy mine to the main feed and cross-post them to Facebook).
- You can have either a TikTok with your author name (@steffanieholmeswrites) or a passion page about a specific trope (@bullyromancerecs). Passion pages are designed to look like readers recommending books.
- The first thing you should do is train your algorithm to put you in bookish content by following lots of booktok people and liking, saving, and commenting on book content on your FYP/main feed. Look for readers who post booktok content about your genre (I do this by searching the titles of my comp books or my comp authors on the platform) and follow them. When you're following around 60-80 creators, you'll start to be recommended only book content in your FYP (For You Page) or main feed. If I see any non-booktok videos on my FYP, I tag them as "not interested".
- You need to decide on a strategy for short-form video content and be prepared to change that strategy as the algorithm changes, which is every month it seems.
- You can show your face in your videos and talk to readers, do lip-syncs and dances to popular sounds, and just be a goof. I try to do these as often as I can because I think it helps readers to get to know me as a person.
- You can also do a type of video called an aesthetic or a "book flip". These are videos with your books

displayed in a background (usually with the covers hidden or pages out so people can't see the cover - some research has shown this works better). You may have a candle flickering or be flipping through the pages of a book to create movement. On top of this scene, you will overlay a catchy hook or scene from your book. The easiest way to explain these is for you to go and look at them. You can check out my main feed – I do two of these a day for different books.

- Another type of content that's popular is 'slides' - photo slideshows (usually of the same photo) with a hooky scene from the book written out one line at a time on each slide.

- You ideally want to be posting once a day, using trending sounds. You can repeat the same hooks/works/videos over and over and over again. I have around 10-20 hooks for each book that I keep repeating, often changing the words slightly or adjusting the hook to work with a current trend.

- These aesthetic videos are all about introducing your books to new readers. They often work better on average than videos with your face, although you are not building a following in quite the same way. For this reason, I do a mixture of both.

- Keep trying things, and use the FYP/feed to see what others are doing and if you can create your own spin on things. Recently, photo slideshows have been working well for people, but that might've changed before I publish this book!

- I use a US sim card in a Tiktok-only phone because I live in New Zealand, and Tiktok is currently tied to your location so it will show your videos to people in your location first and then they'll go out to other countries if the algorithm likes them. I am tricking my phone into thinking I am in the US because the majority of my readers are in the US. However, we're currently counting down to the US Tiktok ban, so we don't yet know the impact this is going to have. I may go back to being a loud and proud New Zealand-based content creator.

- I try to do a couple of silly videos a week with my face that relate to my books. I do a lot of book memes and some packing videos. I alternate these with aesthetic videos or slides.

- I use props to make my aesthetics look magical and mystical, so they fit my brand.

- You don't have to be perfect! Short-form videos love a hot mess. Videos tend to do better when you show up with no makeup and your hair a total shambles. So don't be afraid to be your authentic self. The algorithm can reward that! It's really cool.

- Readers who love short-form video content also love print books and they LOOOOOOVE object/typography covers, especially if they're a luxe edition with foil or sprayed edges or other pretty things. If you have these, show them off in your vids.

- Do not worry about your number of followers. I have very few followers and I have still gone viral a couple of times. Your very first video can go viral. The key is to pack those videos with tropes that readers love.

- The best way to find out how to make short-form video content work for you is to watch heaps of videos, see what sounds and hooks go viral, and rework them for your books.

- My *Poison Ivy* book was written based on TikTok trends. I tested scenes in Tiktok videos before I wrote them – if they performed well, I wrote the scene and made it a big deal in the book. If not, I quietly discarded them. I've started testing scenes as I write on all my books now.

- My last few releases have had a TikTok campaign that started at least a month in advance promoting the book. Some people start even further out and have had it pay off. Get people excited for a book even when it's not out yet!

- Instagram has risen and fallen in popularity over the years. The main feed has been pretty meh for a long time now, but their Reels feature – designed to make Tiktok shake in its boots – has given the platform another jolt of relevancy. I repost my Tiktok videos to reels by using a tool called Snap Tik to remove the Tiktok watermark (or vice versa, using Snap Insta to download a Reel for reposting). I do way better on reels than on Tiktok, but it takes 4 views on a reel to equal 1 view on Tiktok. If I have a video on TikTok that gets to 5k views, I see a little spike in sales. On Reels, I need to get over 20k views to see the same spike.

- Also, the algorithm on Reels is not quite as nuanced as TikTok. I get a lot of mean comments on reels, especially on my darker books. Most of those comments are from people who are very clearly not my audience as they don't like romance novels. So just be aware of that. I don't post my dark contemporary books on reels anymore – only my paranormal. I don't need that nonsense in my life!

- Instagram is a bit more aesthetically focused so images and reels tend to be more polished. I get a lot of followers from Instagram reels and unlike TikTok, followers do still mean something on Instagram, so work on putting more fun author content up on your main feed and in your stories to entice them to keep clicking / reading.

As I said, I'm not a short-form video expert, so these are just a few tips to get you started. It's a super fun platform, I absolutely love it, and they are big fans of my romance books, so hooray. Give it a go, you might be surprised!

FACEBOOK

If you read this book when I first put it out in 2019, I talked a lot about the importance of Facebook. Back then, Facebook was how so many reverse harem readers found their next book to devour. Authors had a huge amount of success by being active in reader groups and by encouraging readers to join their personal author fan groups, where they could tease and tempt readers into picking up their next book.

That's changing.

It's more difficult to gain visibility on Facebook. I used to have a Facebook author group with over 2000 members. When I posted, I was lucky if 10 people saw the post unless I used the @everyone tag. But now everyone uses the @everyone tag, which means it's diminished in effectiveness.

I deleted my Facebook group in 2022. It was a huge relief for me because I've never been able to post and interact there the way I needed to get it rolling. Ever since I deleted my group, I've been doing way better on Instagram, and my Facebook author page is actually pretty active and chatty.

The large genre reader groups are still on Facebook and still active, but they suffer from the same visibility issues.

Facebook isn't what it once was. But there is still some visibility to be had, and if you're an old millennial like me it's probably the platform you're most comfortable with. Genre Facebook groups are still a great place to introduce yourself to the community, and I still love Facebook for networking with other authors. I suggest you join some of the biggest groups and apply for a slot for a takeover (this is where you have exclusive posting rights in the group for an hour to introduce readers to your new book). These will help alert readers to your work. They won't be as effective now as they were three years ago, but if you're new to the genre and self-publishing, those early readers count.

They are also a good place to ask for readers who might be interested in reading an ARC of your book and leaving early reviews. Just make sure you don't fall foul of the group rules on self-promotion!

The more you interact on your author Facebook page or Facebook group, the more your posts will be shown. Welcoming new people to the group, asking questions, creating polls, using tags, NOT using links in your posts, and splashing eye-catching images (I find memes work 100x better than actual promo images, but YMMV) all help increase views and visibility.

Also, if you have your own Facebook reader group or page, don't forget to alert them about your release! Your fans want to know when you've written something new, even if not all of them will follow you into reverse harem.

You can also use Facebook to run ads targeting new readers. Facebook ads are a steep learning curve and I would recommend holding off on using them until you have a deeper understanding of the genre and your goals as an author – focus on getting the packaging of your book right first and getting all the bits and bobs in place (a mailing list, your social media, etc).

I am not a FB ads expert and I have someone who runs these for me. So I won't give any advice on them here, except to say that they are one of the main factors that have carried me from a low six-figure author to a seven-figure author. There will come a point in your author career when you will need to explore pay-per-click advertising.

You can find lots of great books, courses, and groups out there that will teach you how to rock FB ads.

SOCIAL MEDIA

Post about your book on all your social media – whichever social media you enjoy. (If you're new to social media, you can choose one platform and focus on that).

I'm not just talking about posting one single post. I mean multiple posts across *at least* two weeks – telling people all sorts of things about the launch, sharing excerpts and quotes, telling them about the research you've done, asking them questions (this is the best thing because people just want to talk about themselves on social media so it creates engagement), and getting them to play silly games. I usually get the best engagement from polls or observations about pop culture that relate to my audience.

Another thing I like to do once the book is live is create a 'spoiler discussion post' for people who've read the book to talk about all their feels. This works well because my books end on whopper cliffhangers so readers have opinions and theories.

You're trying to entice potential readers and current fans with your characters, setting, and/or hooky story conflicts so they absolutely MUST read your book.

AMS ADS

AMS ads are pay-per-click ads operated by Amazon. They allow you to bid against other authors for better placement in search results, in the 'sponsored products' section located on each book product page, and on the lockscreens of Kindles.

AMS ads can take a lot of fiddling to figure out. Your first step is to compile keyword lists of book titles, authors, and keyword searches related to your books. Look for similar authors and keywords – the books you've found from studying the market. Once you have this list of authors and keywords, you can test different ads with a small budget ($3-5 per day). Over time you will start to notice what works and what doesn't.

Again, I'm not an Amazon ads expert so I won't chime in with tips. I currently don't run these ads, but I have in the past with some success. There are heaps of awesome people out there with books, courses and groups to help you.

GIVEAWAYS

In the early days, with I first started writing whychoose, I had success running themed giveaways based on details from my books. For example, I ran this mega giveaway to celebrate the final book release in the Briarwood Witches series. I included a gift from every character that suited their personality.

Picture: Social media image of the items in my Briarwood Witches mega swag giveaway.

I use the site King Sumo (kingsumo.com) to set up the giveaway. I usually run them for 3-4 weeks. On King Sumo, participants can get additional entries for completing different tasks. I offer additional entries for people who visit the book's page on Amazon, sign up for my mailing list, join my author group, and follow me on Instagram. Each time I run one, I add a few hundred new people on each of those platforms.

I send these giveaways out to my mailing list and promote them on my Facebook page (and my group when I had one), other social media, and on my blog. I also asked other authors if I could add the giveaway to their Facebook groups. Then I can announce the release of my new book on those platforms and capture readers' attention.

This is a simple thing you can do to introduce readers to your new book or series. It also feels like a reward for fans.

Another thing you might try is giving away paperbacks of your book alongside paperbacks of other bestselling authors in your genre – this will draw on their readers who want to win and show them your book is similar.

HOST AN IN-PERSON LAUNCH PARTY

Consider this carefully, as you may end up spending a lot of money on a venue, food, entertainment, etc, but not make up much in sales. Events and book launches are usually attended by your family and friends unless you already have a big following. It's a celebration for you and all the hard work of getting your book out. In terms of sales, they work best if you have a large existing audience and can build an event around the launch that isn't just 'mingle and talk about my book.' Entice your fanbase in with entertainment, great speakers, etc, then hit 'em with your book table as soon as they come in the door.

Another way to sell books is to raise your ticket price but give every ticket holder a free book.

MORE QUICK LAUNCH IDEAS AND TIPS

- Immediately after you hit publish, you'll have to
wait anywhere from 20 minutes to 3 days for your
book to go live on the various storefronts. Once you
see your pretty book is live, you should probably
first purchase a copy and check that it all looks
good – that all the chapters are present and
accounted for. Then, if you haven't already done so,
you'll want to update your multilink and website
(if you have one… hint: you should have one!) with
a page for your book and a BUY NOW button.
After that, you can start putting your launch plan
into action.

- Contact local media about your books. Remember
that writing a book isn't news. You need to tie it to
a wider interest story. I received lots of media for
my children's picture book because I tied it into
statistics about bullying in schools and my own
experiences.

- Put together a leaflet showcasing your book and
hand it out to local libraries. You may also need to
look at listing your books with companies that sell
to libraries. Making librarians aware of your book
can help you get stocked and encourage them to
talk you up to their patrons.

- Put an earlier book in your series on sale. I will
often put book 1 in a series free or on sale for $0.99
during book 3 or 4's launch. I will then use
newsletter services like BookBub, Booksends,
Bargain Booksy, The Fussy Librarian, etc, to let
potential new readers know the book is on sale.

- Run Facebook ads or AMS ads. PPC ads allow you
to target readers who like a similar book or fandom.
For example, when I launched a new book in the

Nevermore Bookshop Mysteries series – which features the character James Moriarty from the Sherlock Holmes books – I targeted fans of the BBC Sherlock series. I wrote ad copy that said things like, "What to read about Sherlock…" These were my most successful ads because they spoke directly to an existing fanbase.

- Post in Facebook groups for your genre. This technique works best when you're already an active member of the groups and you create discussions with lots of engagement.
- Social media takeovers. During these events, you will go to another author's social media page (with their permission, obviously) and 'take it over' with your own posts, games, and competitions. Their readers will participate, and if your book appeals, they may give it a try. The more closely your books align, the more readers you'll likely pick up from takeovers.
- Online parties. Similar to takeovers but hosted on your social media profiles, you'll invite other writers to come along to do games and competitions. They'll bring along a few of their readers each time, and in between their takeovers, you can do your own games and promote your books.
- Go live. Go live on TikTok, Instagram, or Facebook and celebrate your launch live with fans.
- Ask other authors in your genre to promote your book to their readers. Collaborating with other authors in your genre is one of the quickest ways to build new fans. Self-publishing isn't a zero-sum game – a reader can enjoy my book and also a book by my friend. They read so much they don't have to choose. I link her new release in my newsletter and

she does the same to me. We all win. The ability to build these support networks with other authors in your genre is why it's a good idea to start participating online before you launch.

- Set up podcast interviews. A great idea for non-fiction authors in particular, but it would work equally well for fiction. Find podcasts that talk about subjects related to your books. For example, true crime podcasts might be a great fit not just for true crime books, but for mystery writers. Contact the hosts and ask if they'd be interested in having you as a guest. Talk up how awesome you are and say that you've just released a book. It also helps if you're a fan of the show and can gush about it.

- Create YouTube content. YouTube is where most people are finding online content these days. Create videos about aspects of your book and upload them, with a link to your book in the notes, of course! This works great for non-fiction authors who are teaching something that will improve a reader's life. Poets might like to set their poems to music (even cooler if it's music you've created) and post live clips from slams.

- Court book content creators. Bookstagrammers, booktokers, and booktubers are readers who create amazing content about reading and sharing their favourite books, and they often are happy to talk about new indie books they're excited about. Content creators love receiving PR boxes, which they unbox on camera to reveal pretty books and exclusive merch. Some PR companies manage bookstagram campaigns for you, but you may prefer to find potential partners yourself.

A NOTE ABOUT PAID ADVERTISING

There are two main types of paid advertising authors do for their books.

Discount newsletter advertising: Many services offer readers the ability to sign up for a daily email of free or discounted books in their genre. BookBub is the largest and most successful – their featured book ads can cost upwards of $800, but you're likely to sell thousands of books. But there's also Bargain Booksy, Booksends, The Fussy Librarian, etc.

As an author, you can pay a fee to have your free or discounted book pushed out to these readers on a certain date. To be included, your book has to be discounted, and it needs to be approved by the newsletter organizer.

PPC (pay-per-click) advertising: These are Amazon, Facebook, and BookBub ads. (Yes, the same Bookbub that runs paid newsletter ads also does PPC advertising. They have some other cool features, too, such as free author profiles readers can "follow" that will send out an email when you have a new release. You should totally set yourself up as an author on Bookbub just for that). They aim to introduce your book to new readers, and you don't have to run a discount to use these ads, making them great for a launch. You can target readers who like similar authors (or even TV shows in the case of Facebook ads – you have lots of options) and you'll only be charged when someone clicks on your ad.

It's easy to waste a lot of money with PPC ads. My advice is to look at paid ads as something to add to an already successful launch. In the long term, you're going to want to learn how to run great ads, so you might like to experiment with a small budget.

Check out Adam Croft on the Creative Penn podcast and Brian D. Meeks' Mastering Amazon Ads book if you're ready to get started thinking about ads.

HOW TO ROCK YOUR BOOK LAUNCH:

- Psych yourself up. Put on a wicked soundtrack of awesome tunes that'll melt your face off. You wrote a book – and that's amazing! – and now you are gonna bring it to the world!
- Make a plan. Decide all the things that need deciding – pre-order or no pre-order. KU or wide. Formats for launch? How will you get reviews? What will you focus on?
- Find your ARC reviewers if you're using them, and send them your book!
- What's your budget for your launch? You can do lots of awesome work on a launch budget of nil. I used to frequently launch books into the top 3,000 on Amazon with a $0 budget. I have an established audience, so there's that, but by and large, I've built that audience without spending a ton of money. So don't feel as though you have to spend money. But if you have money to spend, you need to know how much it is so you can put it to the best use.
- Do the things on your launch – contact book reviewers, local newspapers, libraries, Facebook groups, and anyone else you think might be interested. Prioritize the stuff on your list according to what's easiest to do and what will create the biggest impact, and just… do the thing.
- Connect with other authors in your genre. Is there a way you can work together to promote each other's books?
- Create a plan for two weeks' worth of social media posts – one week before launch, and one week after launch. You can do more, but that's a good start. You can write and schedule them all in advance if you want to. (I'm rarely that organized).

- Make some graphics for your social media. You can just use your cover photo, but you might like to make some other graphics, too. Try Canva.com for free templates – I love to use funny quotes from the book for Instagram posts. Authors also love graphic sites like Mockup Shots and Book Brush – you upload your book cover and it will add it to lots of awesome images and ad templates.
- Book any promo sites you intend to use.
- Send out a newsletter to remind everyone your book is coming soon.
- It's launch day! Do a dance! Drink or eat something delicious! Put on your awesome soundtrack! And don't forget to send a newsletter to your readers and remind your ARC team to leave their reviews.
- Update your website and anywhere else you need with your live book link.
- If you've organized an in-person event, you should probably attend it. Wear something fierce. Smile a lot. Don't apologize every time someone congratulates you – you wrote a book and you deserve praise!
- It's a week later! Do another reminder to your ARC team to leave their reviews. Bask in the glory of published authordom.
- Start writing your next book!

CHAPTER 9
TURN NEW READERS INTO SUPERFANS

NOW THAT YOU'VE put a book out into the world, you're going to start acquiring readers.

This may happen slowly, or you may suddenly discover yourself in possession of many readers and no clue what to do with them. (an awesome problem we all wished we had!)

After readers have read a book they love, what do they want to do?

- Share and discuss it with other readers.
- Go all giggly and fan-personey over the writer.
- Find out if there's anything else in that world they can devour, or failing that, any other books by the same writer they can enjoy.

To grow your audience and to build a successful career, you need to get your book in front of more readers, make sure it looks hot AF so those readers pick it up, make sure the inside is also hot AF so they love it, and then you need to create *fan spaces* where your readers can go after they finish your book to find out more and stick with you.

We've covered how to do the first three things in previous chapters. In this chapter, we're going to look at ways you can help readers become *fans*.

The more you engage readers between releases, the more likely you'll 'convert' them into fans who buy everything you write.

The internet makes reader engagement incredibly easy. You can build an online community on the cheap – it doesn't cost anything to start a Facebook group or a mailing list. It also means you don't have to leave the house and socialize with strangers in person – a fact for which I am eternally grateful.

Some books will tell you, 'You need a Facebook group,' 'You've got to be on X!' or 'Instagram is the next big thing for authors!' I'm *not* going to tell you that, because I don't think it matters so much what platform you choose for your reader community. It's more important **that you have one**, and that you learn to be a community facilitator who can make that space feel safe, fun and engaging for your crew.

A friend of mine once said to me, "People are on social media because they want to talk about themselves." This is SO TRUE and it completely changed the way I viewed my social media engagement. Instead of just giving announcements, I try to give my readers a chance to talk about themselves in a way they couldn't outside my community. I give them a space they feel they need to be themselves and to be heard.

What kind of fan spaces can you create for your readers?

- A website – A website is a hub for your online presence, as well as a point of information for readers wanting to know more. Your website will list your published books, any in-person appearances, a bio about you, and contact information (you don't have to make your email address available to readers, but it's good to have some way for people to contact you in case a publisher wants to offer you a six-figure book deal). It might also include bonus content, like deleted scenes or a fan shop.

- A social media profile – Here's the thing about social media; it feels as though it's all about you posting pictures of your WIP or your dinner or your cats or whatever, but actually if you want to be good at social media you need to make your profile *about your readers*. Choose whichever platform you enjoy – because if it feels like a chore then that'll come through. No matter which platform you choose, the rules are the same – the more interaction you have on your profile the more you'll be seen and shown to new readers and the more your reach will grow. How do you get readers to interact? MAKE IT ABOUT THEM. Ask questions that get them to talk about themselves. Run competitions that encourage answers. Give them short-form videos that make them laugh or relate to them as readers. Give them polls and ask for their opinion. Show them what you're creating FOR THEM. Issue challenges. Share their posts and replies (with permission).
- A fan group – A fan group is a community space where readers can post about their love of a book, ask questions, discuss spoilers, and maybe win stuff or get cool bonuses. As of the date of publication, most fan groups are on Facebook because that's where readers spend a significant portion of their time online. (This is the reason FB ads for readers are still so effective). This is changing, and many authors do well with fan

groups on other platforms, such as Discord and Circle.

- A mailing list – This is more of an old-school thing, but many authors still get insane engagement from readers through their mailing lists. It's also one of the best things to build because, unlike a social media page where algorithms could change in a flash, you own the data.
- A Patreon (or other subscription services) – The idea of Patreon is that readers invested in your work agree to patronise you for a certain amount of money each month, and in exchange, they get to be part of an inner circle with access to secret extra things. Those extra things might be reading books chapter-by-chapter as they're written, serialised stories that aren't published anywhere else, behind-the-scenes stuff, exclusive art, ARC copies, exclusive special editions, etc.

My Patreon – https://www.patreon.com/SteffanieHolmes Writes – is my fan club. I don't run mine the way others do. Most of my patron content is free – it's the things I might talk about in a Facebook group if I had a Facebook group. I have only one paid tier and there are no physical rewards. For $9 a month, my Raven tier patrons get one chapter of a book (it's called Plot and Bothered, and is book 1 of my popular Nevermore Bookshop series retold from the POVs of the three heroes), ARC copies of all books, early cover and blurb reveals, and occasional special things only for them like podcasts where I answer questions. This is my main fan space, but I try to provide content for fans in other places like my newsletter and social media, too.

Let's look at the most important of these – a mailing list – in more depth. I'll also share with you some of the techniques I use to build fandom with my readers, especially between releases. This is more important for me than ever now that I am on a traditional publishing timetable.

BUILDING A MAILING LIST

A strong, reader-focused mailing list will be one of your best assets for building a fandom. There are three reasons for this:

- Email is a direct line into your readers' lives. You don't have to rely on them going to FB and seeing your ads or heading over to your website. You can hit them in a place they check every day.
- Your mailing list is owned and operated by you. You may use a provider to send the emails but the actual list – the data – is yours. That's powerful because it means you're not at the whims of Amazon or Facebook or Instagram changing policies or visibility.
- Email newsletters have a high conversion rate. They are one of the cheapest and easiest ways to reach the people who've already decided they like you. A key marketing principle is that it's much easier to sell something to a person who likes you. That's why newsletters work so well.

There's no right way to do newsletters. You can do something totally basic – a link in the back of your book for anyone wanting updates, and then you just send a quick email every time you publish a book. Great! That's still 10x better than not having a mailing list in the first place.

Or you can get more complex and use automation sequences, groups, drip campaigns, freebies, A/B testing, and other marketing tools to make your newsletter super effective. I don't want to get into that too much in this book because it's a whole other topic (and also a bit dry and not rock'n'roll).

But I *do* want to touch on the bare basics of setting up a newsletter.

I've outlined five steps. If you can knock off all five of these, then you'll have a functioning newsletter you can send out whenever you have a new release. This is the absolute basic bare-bones of what you'll want to do, but I think anyone can achieve this. Anything extra you do is up to your skill level and enthusiasm.

Here's what you need to do:

- Decide what you want – how often to send your newsletter, what's it going to contain, regular or sporadic, what will it look like?
- Choose your platform – I use a platform called Kit. Many authors like Mailchimp, Mailerlite, or SendInBlue. There are lots of options, and most allow you to build a small list for free.
- Build your initial emails – use the templates on your platform to create a sign-up sequence to conform to privacy laws and introduce yourself and your books (someone who signs up from the back of your book will be familiar with the work they just read, but they don't know you or any of your other books).
- Create a form – so people can sign up.
- Stick your form in lots of places! – on your website, as a pop-up, at the beginning and end of your books.

That's it! You've set up a newsletter. Now you're ready to send out emails.

First, a note about where to promote your newsletter. At the minimum, you should place a link at the front and back of your books. Smarter people than me have tested this and found that the best places to capture readers are in the front of your book and at the end, right after you've written THE END – don't even make them turn the page, just give them the link. You can test this on your books and see where you get the best results.

You should also have your website signup ALL OVER YOUR WEBSITE. You can't go too nuts here. Seriously, some people have websites that are literally JUST their form. This is okay. You can also do a floating popup that appears when a person clicks on your site. I know they're annoying, but people use them because they're so effective.

You can also add your newsletter link to your Amazon author bio, and talk about it in your reader group or on social media. Put it on the back of your business cards. Get it tattooed. Go nuts.

NEWSLETTER CONTENT

Right now, you've got a basic bare-bones organic newsletter. Readers will discover the link at the back of your books and sign up. You'll contact them when you have a new release. It will grow slowly but steadily, and you'll see some okay results.

What if you created the kind of newsletter readers are *excited* to get in their inbox? What if you could get more readers to open your newsletter every time you send it and read more of your books? You want to encourage as many readers as possible to sign up because your newsletter makes them feel special and happy and amazing. And while they're at it, they will buy all the things.

Authors usually use a freebie to encourage more readers to sign up for their newsletter. We discussed this a little in the launch chapter. You've got lots of different options for the freebie you create. Some of the most popular include:

- Companion novella
- An entire book
- An extended epilogue (A little tip from me to you, call it a bonus scene – readers will tear you a new one in the reviews if you call it an epilogue)
- Bonus scenes from anywhere in the book. I love to do these from another character's POV. Readers especially love sex scenes from the guy's POV.
- Extended or deleted scenes, like movie extras
- Alternate endings
- Character interviews
- Detailed family trees
- Maps, artwork, or other visuals of the world
- Behind-the-scenes secrets
- Activity sheets for children's books
- A bonus video or audio download

With freebies, you can also use sites like BookFunnel or Prolific Works for delivery and to help get your freebie noticed by more people.

Now that you've got readers on your list, what will you talk to them about and how often will you email? These decisions differ for every author. Experiment and test.

I will say that one important function of your newsletter is to make sure readers don't forget about you. If you're a writer publishing one book a year, then emailing out once every 1-2 months is a great way to keep readers interested between releases, especially if you've got sneak peeks, bonus content or competitions.

I try to send out my newsletter once per week. I find that because I have a huge backlist and a lot of diversification I never run out of news and content to share. I don't do a specific day because I can't handle the structure.

As for what to write about, here are some ideas:

- New releases
- Pre-orders
- Cover reveals. Cover reveals are great exclusive content, and a good excuse to email and mention an upcoming release.
- Special price promotions, such as a book on sale for $0.99. Sometimes I don't bother sending these out so readers don't get in the habit of waiting for sales. I use sales to hook new readers.
- Author events, such as signings or writer's festivals.
- Launch of new formats (eg. paperback or audio now available)
- Giveaways
- Bonus content
- Games. A lot of my author friends are using sites like BuzzFeed to make quizzes about their books (which hero is for you? What book to read next?)
- Recipes, especially if they relate to the book in some way. I had a book that was about a bakery owner and the month of launch I sent out emails with recipes from the bakery. Those were popular!
- Links to blog posts or other fan content. For example, I wrote a post about priest holes in English castles in my Patreon fan club (because there's a naughty scene in a priest hole in my book) and linked that in my newsletter. This encourages readers to sign up for the Spookybat Fanclub on Patreon.
- Book recommendations.
- Writing updates. Some authors use fun graphics to show how far through a book they are.
- Animal updates. The author HY Hanna has a cat, Muesli, who is named after a cat in her books. So every newsletter she gives a Museli update.

Some writers also like to include personal stories about themselves, TV shows, the writing life, thoughts about the genre, etc.

If that all sounds overwhelming and complicated, don't worry about it. If it's not fun for you, don't do it. I get a kick out of making awesome stuff for readers, but you might prefer to focus your energy on writing the next book.

PATREON

Authors using fandom tools like Patreon and Ream are becoming more common, so I thought I'd mention them briefly.

When I got rid of my Facebook group, I decided I wanted a place where I could funnel readers who were ready to become fans. I've always loved blogging (I had a heavy metal blog for years before I started writing vampire smut) and I love the idea of having an online "fan club" the way my favourite bands did in the 90s. So my Patreon was born.

Most authors use Patreon as a platform for readers who want to go deeper. They will offer bonus content – usually some kind of serialised story or chapters of their WIP – as well as physical rewards like stickers, art cards, and signed paperbacks or special edition books.

I run my Patreon – the Spookybat Fanclub – slightly differently from most authors. The majority of my content is free, and I update several times a month with little articles, voice rambles, book updates, spooky stories, polls, and more. I have a single paid tier – the Raven tier – at $9 a month, no physical stuff, just a monthly chapter, ARC copies of all books, early cover reveals, and a few random bonuses. Patreon posts are often more likely to land in the main inbox than posts from my newsletter, and I love the combination of long-form content, fandom spaces, and 'art patronage', so that's why I'm focused there for the foreseeable future.

The main thing to remember with Patreon is that you need to have an audience before you start one, because it's for fans – it's not a discovery tool. Plan your tiers carefully because you're locking them in. It's better to start with fewer tiers, see how you manage them, and add more later.

SPECIAL EDITIONS AND MERCH

Special editions and merch are fan service that can also be a draw to attract new readers. This is one of the reasons I've gone hard with them in the last few years. The other reason is PRETTY BOOKS.

The special edition book craze has gained some serious traction in the last few years. It's obvious why – PRETTY BOOKS. These books look good in videos, and videos have spread the news about awesome books.

Special editions of your most popular books can be a great way to give. You're also offering a higher-end product that should, if all goes well, have a better profit margin than ebooks. You may find that even if you can't make paid advertising on your ebooks work, paid advertising on special editions returns a sweet profit.

I use offset printers overseas (China, US, Australia) for my special editions. You need to have a minimum of 300 books (sometimes 500) in a print run to make this truly cost-effective. Otherwise, you can do some excellent shorter runs or POD special editions. They might not be able to have all the fancypants things (POD and short runs usually won't have printed edges, foil, or fancy cover treatments, but sometimes they can! It all depends on what your supplier can offer or what workarounds you can find) but you can still do lots of cool things.

A special edition might include any of the following:

- A brand new cover design (perhaps a limited edition).
- Colour or B/W illustrations.
- Colour or B/W chapter headers or heading pages
- Unique internal formatting.
- Maps or diagrams.
- Naked hardcover.
- Dust jacket (single-sided or reversible).
- Foiled details on naked hardcover or dust jacket.
- Signed by the author.
- Spot gloss.
- Embossing.
- Ribbon bookmark.
- Illustrated or coloured endpapers.
- Printed, sprayed, or forced edges.
- Duplex printing.
- Black or coloured pages (often with white or other-coloured ink).
- Raised bands on the spine.
- Different materials for cover (leather, velvet, linen, etc).
- Slipcase.
- Pop ups.

You can do many of these (forced edges, colour illustrations, duplex printing, maps) through POD companies like Ingram Spark. If you want foil, but your print company doesn't do it, you may be able to have foiled dust jackets printed somewhere else and wrap them around your print books.

Authors sell their special editions at events, through their website, through a Kickstarter or crowdfunding campaign, or in limited print runs using a service like Beventi to take pre-orders.

As for merch, the opportunities are endless. I have found

that readers tend to spend their money on the books over merch (we rarely get orders that are just merch, for example), but we've done a lot of creative merch that readers seem to enjoy, including pins, stickers, metal bookmarks, candles, coasters from the pub in my books, a newspaper from the village in my books, postcards, SFW and NSFW art cards, and plushies.

HOW TO ROCK YOUR FANDOM:

- Think about where your peeps hang out. What platforms do they use? Are they on FB, Instagram, Discord, Slack, or Twitch?
- Think about where you enjoy hanging out online. Can you find a way to make a welcoming space for readers? Choose your social media / fan group profiles based on an intersection of what your readers like and what you enjoy.
- Build a simple website and add all your books. Urgh, I know. It's annoying. But once it's done you won't have to do it again. Hopefully forever. Or at least until the internet no longer exists. WordPress, Wix and Squarespace are good platforms to try.
- Make a mailing list. Urgh, I know. It's also annoying. But once it's done you won't have to do it again. Well, you will have to update it and send out mail to your readers, but how much and how often is up to you. Do what feels comfortable for you.
- Ask questions and get readers to talk about themselves. This will improve your engagement and make your social media platforms more popular.
- Is there a fun thing you can make for your fans? This could be as simple as a short story or postcard

from the world of your books, or as fun and involved as a special edition.

- Enjoy talking with your readers! They are awesome people who think you're just the coolest person. It's a nice ego trip. You are a rockstar of words!

CHAPTER 10
FIND A STRATEGY THAT WORKS FOR YOU

YOU'VE DONE IT! You're an author. A rockstar of words. (A wordstar, if you will). You have a book that you've written out in the world. That's actually amazing. Now, when people ask you what you've been up to at a party, you can say, "Well, I just published this book," and whip out a copy to show them.

Totally not weird at all.

Right now, you're probably focused hard on trying to get more people to buy your book. That's great. But as an indie author, you're now officially part of the indie author community, which means you're going to be in spaces where people share a LOT of information about what works – and doesn't – for their books.

Indie authors are extremely generous about sharing their experiments, case studies, and 'here's what worked for me.' The problem is, all this information can leave you feeling as if you have to do a million things. And that's not true.

I don't want you to feel overwhelmed or that being a successful indie author is impossible because you aren't able to juggle writing 10 books a year and social media and ads and a special edition Kickstarter and managing a Patreon and and and…

There are endless different configurations of strategies you can use. The only strategy I recommend is the one that works for you. But you're probably going to have to experiment with different things to figure out what that is.

When I used to coach authors, we would work on creating a 12-month strategy that was tailored to each author's strengths, what they enjoyed doing, and where they were likely to see the biggest wins with their particular readership.

Strategies for a sustainable author career could be a whole other book (maybe it will be one day. It's one of my favourite topics!). I can't possibly give you an exhaustive list. What I wanted to do with this section was show you a few different strategic directions authors commonly use and talk about, so that you can see there are many different approaches to an indie career, and not all techniques work for all strategies.

STRATEGY: YOUR BOOK AS A PLATFORM

This strategy is about using your book as a stepping stone on a path to something bigger that you want.

Being a published author in certain spaces will promote you as an expert. Imagine walking into a job interview and being able to say, "Oh, I wrote a book on this subject." Imagine a recruiter Googling your name and seeing your book on Amazon with lots of glowing reviews!

Many business owners write a book as part of their strategic plan as it will lead directly to new clients. You can use your book to source leads that you'll nurture and funnel into higher-priced items like coaching and courses. Your book can drive traffic and inquiries to an online shop or raise the profile of a brick-and-mortar store. For example, a friend of mine who ran a popular wedding blog wrote and published a wedding planning book. Not only is the book the first product she could sell, but it presented her as an expert in the wedding industry and now she gets invites to all these cool events and exciting brand partnerships.

Another example is my local bakery, who indie published a cookbook that offers them a product to sell while also raising the profile of the baker.

But you don't have to be in business to get cool opportunities because you're a writer. You might be able to wrangle a profile about yourself in the local paper. You can pitch yourself to writers' and readers festivals as a guest speaker (if you love speaking, these can be some absolute career highlights). You can visit schools and get kids excited about reading. You could write articles about your favourite subject and have them published in magazines and other books.

You could expand your book's world into games, movies, swag, colouring books, and any other product you could imagine. Back in 2018, I had my illustrator friend Bree design t-shirts with funny phrases from some of my Nevermore Bookshop characters for a reader shop on my website. Bree used the success of our Kickstarter campaign to launch her own tarot deck. I know other authors who've done colouring books and graphic novels, who've licensed their books as cartoons and movies, and who are writing interactive fiction and radio drama. The possibilities are truly endless.

If you feel called to teach what you've learned, you could help other authors navigate the world of writing craft or self-publishing, or be a ghostwriter for people who don't want to create their own books. You might provide services to authors or readers, such as editing, PR, or managing their social media. There are so many possibilities.

Your book is only the beginning.

STRATEGY: RAPID RELEASE

Rapid release is a launch technique made popular by authors like Michael Anderle and Craig Martelle from the 20BooksTo50k Facebook group. The idea is that the closer together you release books, the more voracious readers you'll capture as they'll be able to immediately binge your series. Also, because Amazon favours newly released books and gives a ranking boost to a new release in its first 30-90 days, many authors find getting more books out during this window will help keep their earnings high.

When authors refer to rapid releasing, there is no set amount of books or time between them, but writing and publishing one book a month would generally be considered a rapid-releasing schedule. For me, I'd consider anything over four books a year a rapid release schedule (which means that I used to rapid release but don't anymore). Some authors will release several books a month as part of their rapid-release strategy.

Rapid release might mean holding back on releasing books until you have several complete, then releasing them at once. BOOM BOOM BOOM.

Usually, authors will hold back 3 books to release either simultaneously (all on the same day) or in succession (once a week or every 2-3 weeks). You might have the 4th book in the series on pre-order and be writing it while you release the others.

Stockpiling and rapid releasing can be a great way to jumpstart a successful brand. The downside is that you will spend a lot of time writing and editing without earning while you stockpile, and if your books end up fizzling (which does happen) you might have invested all that time writing a long series that didn't do well. If you'd known six months earlier that the series wouldn't land, you might have adjusted the plot of your series to finish it in 3 books instead of 7.

We've spoken a little about rapid releasing in the chapter on writing faster. If you need to sell 1000 books a month, the more books in a backlist you have, the easier it will be to hit that number.

A rapid-release strategy relies on the writer being able to get out books fast. Many, many authors have indeed done well from the rapid release strategy, but in some spaces, it's touted as the only way to reach success as an indie. And that's not true.

Rapid-releasing strategies can work well for authors who like spotting trends and carefully studying the market. They may jump around a bit and focus less on read-through to chase the potential big wins of emerging trends and micro-tropes.

I used to use a rapid-release strategy. I would publish 6-8 books a year. This meant I built up a backlist of 50 books relatively quickly. I knew that in a release month, I'd see a spike, so I wanted as many of those spikes in a year as I could get. But as I grew in my career I realised that I didn't have time to launch books the way I wanted. I'd see the spike, but then my sales would drop off to a similar level.

I couldn't seem to push past a certain level of sales and success. I also had not time to nurture my fandom or do cool projects like special editions because I was spending all my time trying to write the next book to deadline.

I was also starting to feel that creating a few months of anticipation between releases is actually better for a great launch.

I slowed down to 3-4 books a year, and I've been very happy with the results. Rapid releasing got me to 6 figures a year, but my new strategy got me to 7.

Rapid releasing authors love: Studying the market. Writing quickly. Digging into tropes and micro tropes. Jumping around different subgenres. Doing the bare minimum marketing. Having a deadline. Big spikeys on their earnings graphs.

STRATEGY: WORLD WEAVING

Authors who adopt a world-weaving strategy (my name for it!) are focused on writing in a world they've created, whether it's a fantastical setting, a small town, or a creepy city. All of their books are set in this world, and their strategy involves immersing readers in the world as much as possible for maximum read-through.

(A world weaver may also focus more on a certain character – such as a long-running crime detective series).

World weavers tend to be fan-focused. They spend a lot of their energy between releases interacting with their audience and creating things to engage readers with their world.

This is where I feel most comfortable, and slowing down my publishing schedule in recent years has allowed me creative space to embrace this and give my fans loads of cool stuff.

World-weaving authors love: special editions, bonus content, expanding the world through merch and events, Kickstarters, a few big projects a year, writing everything in the same world, and talking with fans.

AUTHOR SUPERSTAR STRATEGY

In this strategy, you make the reader so utterly wild for you, the author, that they want anything and everything you put out – no matter if you're writing paranormal romance or sentient octopus poetry.

Authors can do this in several ways. Most commonly, author superstars are found on social media, putting up loads of content and being out there and wild and causing chaos. They focus their attention on amassing a large following, knowing that some of that following will convert to whatever project they're doing next. They will often write something in a hot trend, but put their own spin on it, and they don't usually stick to one theme/genre (but sometimes they do!).

Author superstars love: A few big launches a year. Surprising their audience with something fun. Experimenting. Doing the last thing people expect. Focusing on creating viral and engaging free content to entice fans into their world. Having a wicked amazing personal brand.

CHAOS GREMLIN STRATEGY

This strategy is the throw everything you've got at the wall and see what sticks. The Chaos Gremlin strategy may be adopted by newer authors who are enjoying publishing while they figure out what they want to do, so they're trying a lot of different genres or formats, or it may be adopted by legitimate chaos gremlins who get a big kick out of saying, "You can't tell me what to do!"

Do I advise this strategy? No. If you're a true Choas Gremlin, you're going to adopt it anyway.

Chaos gremlins love: Chaos. Following their muse. Exploring lots of different creative paths (often at the same time).

CASE STUDY: MY STRATEGY FOR THE FANGS FOR NOTHING RELEASE

I published this case study in a couple of author groups, and I wanted to republish it here because I thought it might be useful for you to see how an author can use strategy to help them choose what to focus on.

My books are hard to categorise because they sit in a weird made-up place between genres – they're paranormal, but not in a "normal" way (shifters and vamps), they're kind of cosy mysteries, but they're spicy, they're kind of cosy fantasies, kind of supernatural suspense, kind of romantic comedies, kind of gothic…

(I also had a brief sidetrack into dark romance, which I've discussed in previous chapters. I keep my dark romance books under my same pen name, but I don't promote them as much as my main books.)

Despite the kookiness of my books, I managed to cobble together a mid-six-figure annual revenue as an indie in 2023, which BLOWS MY MIND. I had a viral dark romance hit back in 2019, but apart from that outlier, my launches are pretty chill, none of my books are burning up Tiktok or ranking super high – but I have a lot of books that all do FINE, and a few fun extra projects like Kickstarters that come together to create a wonderful, abundant career. I also live in New Zealand, so getting paid in USD is pretty sweet.

This is all amazing to me! I've been a full-time author for over six years and I still bounce downstairs every morning unable to believe I get paid to do this. I am so incredibly lucky. How cool is author life?

In 2024 I set the goal of my first seven-figure year. I knew that I would be writing the final books in my two main series, and writing 1-2 books in a brand-new series. I knew my main opportunity to leap up my income would be the new series, and also that I would spend the next 2-3 years writing this series, so I spent some time considering the best way to approach it.

PLANNING MY NEW SERIES

Here are some things I considered:

- **I need to be SLIGHTLY less quirky.** My books/style are fun, light and quirky, and I want to retain that but also create something that more romance readers will pick up.

- **I want to build on what I've already created.** My two most popular series are in an interconnected world (a cosy English village where strange things happen and a cursed bookshop) and this world has fans! And I love it there and don't want to leave :) If I build on what I've already created, then I don't have to work so hard to bring in new people AND I have lots of content to give fans if they love the new series.
- **I don't need any new readers to hit my goal** – all I need is for the majority of my current fans to read the new series. I want to focus my efforts on selling this new series to my current people and giving them an amazing fan experience.
- **I have a system in place.** I have all the pieces in place that I need – NL, ads, graphics, etc. Making tweaks to the system is NOT going to get me to my goal. I need to approach this new series assuming the system is fine so I can focus on other areas.
- **I want to write better books.** It all comes back to the books. I want to write a book that's worthy of going viral and getting all the fan love. I want to improve my craft because I know I can write a good book, but I want to write GREAT books, for my readers and for me.

So, with those themes in mind, I came up with a plan for the new series.

- **I created a brand new concept for my new series, set in the same world, in the structure of a traditional romance series.** Each book would feature a different heroine from a book club that meets at my magical bookshop finding their forever love while helping to solve a mysterious supernatural murder across the whole series. You'd meet all the book club members in book 1 so you were invested in waiting for their story.

- **The series would be trope-driven.** I would pick popular romance tropes for each book in the series and research/plan out core scenes that are an essential part of the reading experience of those tropes to include in the books. I would use the tropes as loose structural elements from which I could be as quirky as I liked. (I saw an interview with Ritchie Blackmore - guitarist of Deep Purple who now writes amazing medieval rock music with his wife Candice Night – and he was talking about how he takes these old, traditional medieval songs that have been played for hundreds of years, and puts them into the "Blackmorizing Machine" and comes out with something that respects the song but is fresh and wonderful and uniquely HIM. I want to do the same thing – put beloved tropes through the "Steffmoreizing Machine" and see what comes out.)

- **I'll make this series MF instead of whychoose.** My other two series are whychoose and have done very well, but I decided this series should have a more traditional romance structure. Now, whychoose books are big! Lots of them hit the top 100 (even top 10! Even top 1!) and do insanely well! BUT, it's still a quirk factor and I wanted to remove at least ONE quirk factor so I could be just a SMIDGE more mainstream. I don't want to temper my voice so this is the factor I chose to remove.

- **I'll hire a developmental editor.** I've never worked with one before, and I sort of always had this idea that I didn't need one because my career has proven I know how to write a book. This is the wrong attitude! Becca Syme said something like this at a conference I recently attended. "Instead of spending your time trying to learn how to do all the things you hate and suck at, focus on doing the things you do well BETTER." A developmental editor is a great idea at my level. I met someone amazing at a conference I attended and something about their attitude and love of the genre and heart just screamed THIS WAS MEANT TO BE. I hired them and have loved every moment of working with them, and the book is so much better for it.

- **I will focus my launch on bonus content.** I have never done anything like this before, but I decided to introduce the new series to my current readers through bonus content - much of which references my other two series that they loved. I want them all to be so excited they HAD to read this series.

- **I will allow the system I've already built to do the rest of the work for me.** This launch, I will not read a gazillion articles about new marketing tips to try. I would not organise NL swaps or post the launch in other author groups. I would focus on building this amazing fan experience and see what happens.

So that was the plan. I wrote the book over three months and launched it on September 10, 2024.

WRITING THE BOOK

I knew the book would end up on the long side, because I was writing a whole romance arc, introducing all the other characters in the book club, building a vampire world, AND starting a murder mystery all in one book. I didn't quite anticipate HOW long – 144k words. My longest book ever. Yay! Lots of sweet, sweet KU reads.

You know how some books you have to fight for every. Single. Word. Some books are a pure joy from 'It was a dark and stormy night…' through to 'To be continued.' This book was the latter. I had so much fun writing this!

As I wrote the book, I took scenes I liked and made them into Tiktok slides. I was doing one Tiktok slide deck a day for the length of the launch and racking up a few pre-orders per day. By launch, I had 463 pre-orders, which is the most pre-orders I've had on book 1 of a new series if we don't count my 2019 outlier.

BONUS CONTENT

Because I was writing a vampire book, I was thinking a lot about the OG vampire book, Dracula, which is an epistolary novel. I've done a lot of epistolary content before (text messages, newspaper articles, notes, etc, as part of telling the story), but I wanted to step it up in this series because I think this is something I do well and is part of my voice. So along those lines, I created some epistolary bonus content:

- **Book club invitation:** My designer created an invitation inviting the reader to the first-ever Nevermore book club meeting. Readers could add themselves to a list to get 1 of 100 of these invitations sent to them in the mail. Those went quickly!
- **Group chats:** I wrote a bunch of group chats of the characters in my older main series talking about this new book club starting. My assistant made them into chat videos. They got quite a bit of engagement on TikTok and Insta. I will be doing way more of these!

- **Newspaper and Tourism Guide:** Members of the book club have different jobs around the village – tourism director, chef, yoga instructor, fortune teller, reporter. I wrote a village newspaper with some of them contributing articles and made it my newsletter for the day. I did another newsletter as a tourism guide for my village. I might permanently make my newsletter the village newspaper, still debating this.
- **AITA:** I used a template someone made and posted in a FB group for authors to use to create a Reddit AITA post from the vampire hero of my series. This was so fun. I might do it with all my series.

I disseminated all this content through my Patreon, NL, and social media. (I've spoken about my Patreon in an earlier chapter. I don't run mine like most people – most of my Patreon content is free and I have only one paid tier. All of this bonus content was free).

LAUNCH

I wrote four different blurbs, each from a different character's POV or highlighting a different trope. I had them tested via FB ads. The winner by a longshot is the current blurb - a third-person blurb from the hero's POV (the book is in first person).

I decided to give my readers a schedule of when they could expect certain things. Usually, I just throw this stuff up whenever, but I thought this time I'd be intentional about it.

> *July 9 - pre-order/trope reveal*
> *August 6 - Cover/Blurb reveal*
> *August 15 - You're Invited - 100 free postcards*
> *August 20 - group chat 1*

August 27 - group chat 2
September 3 - Newspaper
September 6 - Tourism Guide
September 9 - group chat 3
September 10 - Launch
September 11 - Release Party/Q&A FB live video
  with me

I had a surprising number of people at my live release party considering that I do not have a FB group (this was done through my page).

I also used Netgalley for the first time. I decided because this was a new series it would be a good idea to try and make sure readers are aware the world exists. To date, I've had over 800 requests and some incredible reviews.

All amounts below are in NZD unless otherwise stated.

I had a $ 10-a-day ad on the book during pre-launch. I ramped up to $100 a day during the launch in the US store (Around $60US I think). I have not turned this ad off or lowered spend since, and I've also just started $10 a day in the UK. The ads use videos from my TikTok.

THE RESULTS

As of right this second (January 2025), the book has made me $80,000, not including my traditional publishing advance. In terms of Amazon's ranking, it peaked in the 700s, dropped back to 1050, and has been hovering between 700-1500 ever since.

Apart from my outlier 2019 series, I have never had a book stay so sticky at such a high ranking for so long.

It's also pushed up the ranking/earnings of my main interconnected series (10 books - the second two images), so that's been a major boost, too. This book enabled me to hit my $1 million goal in 2024.

But I'm excited about more than that. Money is sweet, but I feel as though I've found a strategy that works for me and is enjoyable and manageable. I like that I get to hang out in my quirky world. I'm not looking at what other authors are doing. I'm just thinking of fun stuff to give my fans. I'm leaning into what I do well. And it's working!

HOW TO ROCK YOUR AUTHOR STRATEGY:

- When you read about people's techniques and strategies in author groups or at conferences, ask yourself, "Does this fit with my strategy?" and "Does this excite me?" If not, you don't have to do it! Just because something is working for someone, doesn't mean you have to do it, too.
- When you adopt a new technique, you should also shuffle something off your plate. Your plate is only so big. You can't keep piling stuff onto it.
- Go back to your success metric from Chapter One. Is this still what you're vibing? What strategy will get you there in the funnest way possible?
- Don't be shy about the fact you published a book. It doesn't matter what other people think of your genre – you've done something very few people ever achieve. Celebrate and talk about your experience. It's part of what makes you an interesting person.
- Your book might be only one part of your overall business plan or ultimate goal. If so, what is your ultimate goal? How does that factor into the success metric we worked out in Chapter 1?
- If you're a business owner, think about how you can use your book to leverage into higher-profit and value-add products. This often includes courses, coaching, and membership sites, but it

might be as simple as using your book to raise the profile of your store.

- Add your book to your resume and LinkedIn page. (If it's relevant to your industry). Add it to your professional and personal social media bios. Enjoy the feeling of 'published author' on your tongue.

- Think about the kinds of things you'd like to do as a writer. Do you have any writerly dreams, like speaking at a conference or mentoring young writers? You don't have to wait to be invited – contact a writer's festival about applying to be on the bill (look for localized or genre-focused festivals for your best chance of success), and talk to local schools, writer groups and youth groups about hooking up with awesome young writers. You wanted to write a book, and you made that happen. If you want other things, make them happen, too.

- Plan out your rapid-release schedule, and look at all the cool things you get to create.

- Figure out how you're going to write more in your world, and what bonus content and cool special stuff you want to give your fans.

- Pitch articles and excerpts from your book to magazines, journals, and websites. You can even earn a nice bit of spare change doing this.

- What other products within your book's world might your readers enjoy? Give them something cool.

- Did I mention that you should be celebrating? Seriously. Eat an epic sandwich. Do a Snoopy dance. Buy a yacht. You're rocking it as a self-published wordstar! That's badass.

CHAPTER 11
EXPERIMENT AND HAVE FUN!

PART of what's so amazing about self-publishing and being an indie author is the ability to pivot, try new things, and follow your imagination wherever it leads. You can start a new pen name and try a completely different genre, create multiple formats for your books, co-write or write in a shared world, or team up with other creatives to experiment with new ways of storytelling.

You can do *all the things*. This can be freeing. It can also be a lead weight around your neck, stopping you from moving forward. It can be both at the same time. Humans are complex weirdos.

Yes, do all the things if that makes you happy, but *try* **to stick to a plan.** There's always the temptation to chase a new shiny idea, but always put on your publisher hat and ask if that idea is going to get you closer to your ultimate success.

In 2016 I released a successful first book in a new series. It did so well that I worked my ass off to publish a co-written book with a friend, write a standalone book in a new world, and finish another series under my other pen name. All the while, the readers of that first book were left wondering if the series would continue.

Even though I published a book every two months, it was nearly eight months later before I wrote book 2, and by that time many of those readers moved on. I don't regret those tangent projects, but splitting my focus set me back probably a year from my goal of being a full-time author. Now I finish one series before I start another, and if a shiny idea is calling to me, I might set aside an hour a day to noodle on it instead of breaking away from what I know works.

Always look for new opportunities. I wrote a children's book with a friend, and launched it with a Kickstarter campaign. I work with cool creatives to make and sell my own merch and special editions. I'm currently in talks about doing a graphic novel, and I just signed a traditional publishing contract. While I try to focus on doing more of what works, I pay attention to what's going on in the wider self-publishing world and where I might be able to slide on in and find new readers.

Read indie books and look at how other authors manage their careers. Some of my favourite self-published authors are H. Y. Hanna cosy mysteries), Darcy Coates (haunted house horror), Karpov Kinrade (YA vampire fantasy), C.M. Stunich (reverse harem romance), and Gala Darling (blogger extraordinaire).

And lastly, **don't be a stranger!** Reach out to the amazing community of indie authors across the world. Come join the conversation and share your journey. Share advice, learn from others, and commiserate over creative challenges. Writing can be a lonely pastime, and having a tribe makes it that much more fun.

HOW TO ROCK BEING AN INDIE AUTHOR:

- Make a plan.
- Stick to the plan as much as possible…

- …while also allowing a bit of wriggle room for the Muse.
- Keep an eye on what others are doing and how the industry changes and adapts, but…
- …don't jump on every new thing. Ask yourself if it's a good fit for you FIRST.
- Read lots of awesome books by fellow authors. I know, what a chore, right?
- Join the conversation and use your story to inspire other authors. If we all fly together, nothing can stop us.
- Something.
- Something.
- PROFIT.
- *(Just kidding).*
- *(Sort of).*
- Always, always be raging against the manuscript.

PUTTING IT ALL TOGETHER

You may have got to this point in this book, and you're thinking, "I've got a plan for the rest of my series and I've nailed my author brand and all that jazz, but I don't see how this is going to get me any closer to my goals."

Fair enough. That's why what I'm going to do in this chapter is to show you how all the elements in this book can come together to create the potential for an amazing writerly future.

When you go to your 9-to-5 job, you're exchanging your time for money. You work 40 hours a week and you receive a check for an agreed amount at the end. That amount is fixed – it goes up or down if you change your hours. You might get a pay raise, but generally speaking, your income will stay fixed at around the same amount.

If you have a full-time career as an author, life is very different.

Your books are infinitely scalable. What I mean by this is that you can create a business that sells 1,000 books a month, but that business could grow to sell 10,000 books a month or 100,000 books a month without you needing to put in extra hours or hire more people. (You might choose to do those things, but if your business is scalable, the **process is the same** no matter how many copies you sell). This separates you from this time-for-money exchange.

You can sell ebooks and audio over and over again – there's no inventory to stock and your books will never go out of print. With POD technology, you can even create scalability for paperbacks. You can sell books all over the world, and create other formats like audio. You can license subsidiary rights (film, foreign translations).

Another thing you have at your disposal is data. All the publishing platforms give you instant, real-time access to data that shows you how book sales are going. Many traditionally published authors don't get this visibility. They'll see a royalty statement every six months, so they can't tell what marketing efforts move books. You can see in minute detail what works and what doesn't, and use this data to improve and make tweaks.

No one owes you an audience or a living. You will rise or wither by how much you satisfy readers with your books. That uncertainty can be scary, but for the right kind of people, it's creatively stimulating.

It helps a lot if you have a partner with a normal job and one of those nice, regular paychecks. I'm so lucky that I have a supportive husband who enjoys his government job. He gives us security – if my income takes a nosedive, his income will keep us afloat while I pivot my business (and it has in the past).

Another way to help manage a self-publishing career is to keep your expenses as low as possible. Save money for leaner months. You don't have to be a millionaire to do this. The leaner your expenses, the more freedom you have to enjoy all the awesome stuff money can't buy. Amazing experiences, freedom, wonderful people, creative integrity… all the good stuff.

You get to live a truly unique life. You're an artist, so

people kind of expect you to be a bit strange. Lean into that, because why the hell not? You're heavy fucking metal (or is that just me?)

You will butt heads with gatekeepers. You have two options – you can twist your work to fit what they want, or you can bypass them altogether. Both options have merit, and it comes down to what you want to achieve and what you need to survive. It's never a bad thing to take the payday that supports your family, as long as you stay true to your values.

What I see in my career is a big spike in income when I release a new book, and then over time, that spike will flatten out. But each time I release a book, the spike gets a little bigger and the flatline is a little bit more lucrative. If I'm a $200k a year author after 35 books, and a 7-figure author after 50, where will I be when I've published 75 books? I can't wait to find out.

Being an author can be a bit of a rollercoaster. Sometimes a release won't do as well as you expect, or Amazon will glitch and, say, forget to send out your pre-order book, leading to hundreds of readers complaining and leaving bad reviews. Not that that's happened to me. Not at all. I love Amazon and my benevolent overlord Bezos…

The more frequently you release new content or conduct marketing efforts to grow your audience, the more you'll notice those spikes even out. Now, I'm at the point where I'm releasing something new (even if it's a shorter guide like this) practically every month. This helps my income to regulate across the year. I can better predict what I'm earning and plan for big launches and advertising.

Every book you write adds to your backlist – and that backlist will continue to earn you money for years to come. As I've said numerous times in this book, you set yourself up for success by keeping your backlist as tightly branded as possible, so more readers will binge *everything* you've got. In saying that, as you grow your reader base and your financial cushion, you can afford to take risks and try something different.

I love self-publishing because it's opened me up to the world of entrepreneurship. I feel as though I was born to be an entrepreneur. I love making something, putting it out into the world, and seeing what happens. If you're reading this book, I think you will, too.

And lastly, the best creative inspiration comes from a place of joy and acceptance. If you're not having fun, then ask yourself why that is. Are you excited about your writing? Is something else going on in your life that you need to deal with? Are you still interested in being a writer? It's perfectly okay to take a step back, to change what you're doing, to slow down or speed up, to quit altogether.

You don't have to be miserable to be a great artist. Look after yourself. Deal with your shit. Be kind to others and the earth. Lift up your fellow artists, because this isn't a zero-sum game. Celebrate your successes and your failures. Have an absolute blast!

Write the book. Do the thing. Publish the book. Take over the world.

And always rage against the manuscript.

WHAT TO DO NEXT

The world of indie publishing is overwhelming. I get that. All you wanted to learn was how to publish a book, and I've just bombarded you with a whole ton of ideas and strategies for your career and the future of reading.

In this section, we put everything we've just talked about together to create an action plan to get you from where you are right now to the next rung on the ladder of where you want to be. If you're reading this book because you want a clear path to success, then this is where you map out the beginning of a strategy.

In a very particular order, here's what I recommend you do.

DEFINE WHAT SUCCESS MEANS TO YOU

This is where you sit down and think about what you actually truly want from your writing. Brainstorm. Get creative. Don't be afraid to dream big – but remember, it has to feel authentic to you. It's all very well dreaming about fame and riches, but ask yourself why? Why do you want to be rich? If you don't do something with it, you just have a pile of money. Boring.

No one gets excited about that except maybe bankers and ducks.

Consider what you want to do with your life and the kind of person you strive to be. How do your books factor into that? Put some solid numbers on it – such as the amount of copies you want to sell. Consider the kind of stories you want to be known for – what's your author brand?

TAKE A CRITICAL LOOK AT YOUR ALREADY PUBLISHED WORK

If you've already dabbled with self-publishing, it's time to take an inventory. Look at:

- How many books do you have?
- Are you letting your readers down in any areas?
- Do you need better editing, new covers, or an updated blurb?
- Do you have a cohesive author brand?

THINK ABOUT HOW YOU COULD CREATE A SERIES TO HOOK READERS

How do other authors in your genre tackle series? Can you expand your ideas or world to add series potential?

READ SOME SUCCESSFUL INDIE AUTHORS IN YOUR GENRE

Learn from their triumphs and mistakes. Look at their 'package' – the book itself, the cover, the blurb, the marketing. What's the experience they're giving readers? How can you deliver the same consistent experience?

DEFINE YOUR BRAND

Who are you as an author? What's the one sentence that describes your body of work? What do readers get when they pick up one of your books? Are there any elements of your brand that have been damaged? (For example, bad editing results in lots of low reviews for a book). It's time to get serious and take control of your brand.

START A MAILING LIST

Just do it already! If you do no other marketing for your books at all, you should do the mailing list.

MAKE DECISIONS

KU or wide? 6x9 or 5x8? Facebook or Instagram? Learning about self-publishing can feel so overwhelming. You can be paralyzed by the fear of getting it wrong.

Writers often fall into the trap of trying to crowdsource their business decisions. I am so guilty of this. We have this wonderful online community of fellow authors who seem to know everything, and we feel lost, so we go to them for advice. "Should I be wide or KU?" "Should I have a pen name for this new project?" and we get 100 contradictory answers.

Everyone means well, but they're answering based on their own experience. And this can leave you feeling more lost than ever. You need to let go of the idea of there being a "right" decision and a "wrong" decision. All publishing strategies have merit. It's about which one is right for you. And only you can know that.

So stop crowd-sourcing your business decision. When I feel lost with a decision about my books, I give myself a short timeframe for a decision – "I have ten minutes" or "I have an hour." I read all the information I could find within that time-frame, mull it over, and then at the end, I make a decision. I don't waste any more time on it. I have a path forward, so now I can implement it.

Sometimes that decision is right for me. Sometimes it's wrong. I only learn by doing. Very few decisions are black/white. It's better to get them out of the way and move forward than to wallow in indecisiveness.

DREAM BIG, AND HAVE FUN

For me, this is the most important thing. Being a successful indie author is hard – there are much easier ways to make money. So if you're not having fun, there's no point. You might as well be doing pretty much any other job. Sure, be strategic, think about the market, and focus on your readers, but make sure you're enjoying yourself and you're proud of the stories you tell.

Now, go forth and write! I'll see you on the bestseller charts!

RAGE AGAINST THE MANUSCRIPT

Revised for 2023 with over 10k words of new content. Learn how to write the hottest romance genre... reverse harem!

Reverse harem books are hot in the charts right now. The trope of one woman having multiple male partners is attracting writers from all genres. If you want to write your own reverse harem and create the ultimate wish-fulfilment story where a strong, sassy heroine gets *all* the hot guys, check out this guide by a bestselling six-figure reverse harem author.

You'll learn:

- What readers are looking for in their next reverse harem read.
- How to write sizzling sex between multiple partners.
- Whether or not to include MM in your reverse harem novel.
- A simple 9-step method for plotting your book.
- How to build a successful reverse harem series.

- Popular tropes reverse harem readers love.
- Tips to create a cover that grabs eyeballs (not literally!)
- Marketing your novel to this growing audience, and...
- How to build a thriving long-term writing career!

Filled with tips and examples from Steff's own personal experience, as well as references to popular reverse harem novels, this book will be your essential guide to this hot new genre!

Read now: https://books2read.com/writingreverseharem

ABOUT THE AUTHOR

Under her pen name Steffanie Holmes, Steff is the *USA Today* bestselling author of kooky, spooky paranormal, cozy fantasy, and gothic romance. Her books feature clever, witty heroines, secret societies, quirky villages where nothing is as it seems, creepy old mansions, and alpha males who *always* get what they want.

Legally-blind since birth, Steffanie received the 2017 Attitude Award for Artistic Achievement. She was also a finalist for a 2018 Women of Influence award.

Steffanie lives in New Zealand with her husband, a horde of cantankerous cats, and their medieval sword collection.

Come hang with Steffanie
www.steffanieholmes.com
www.rageagainstthemanuscript.com